PSL MODEL RAILWAY GUIDE

5

Operating your layout

Michael Andress

 PSL Patrick Stephens, Cambridge

First published in 1981

**Also in the same series and by the
same author**
1 Baseboards, track and electrification
2 Layout planning
3 Structure modelling
4 Scenery
6 Branch line railways
In preparation
7 Modern railways
8 Narrow gauge railways

**British Library Cataloguing in Publication
Data**

Andress, Michael
   PSL model railway guide.
   5: Operating your layout
   1. Railroads—Models
   I. Title
   II. Model railway guide
   625.1'9   TF197

   ISBN 0 85059 436 7

Cover photograph by Brian Monaghan
showing a member of the Macclesfield Model
Railway Group at the controls.

Text photoset in 8 on 9 pt Univers by
Manuset Limited, Baldock, Herts.
Printed in Great Britain on 100 gsm Huntsman
Velvet, and bound, by The Garden City Press,
Letchworth, Herts, for the publishers
Patrick Stephens Limited, Bar Hill, Cambridge,
CB3 8EL, England.

Contents

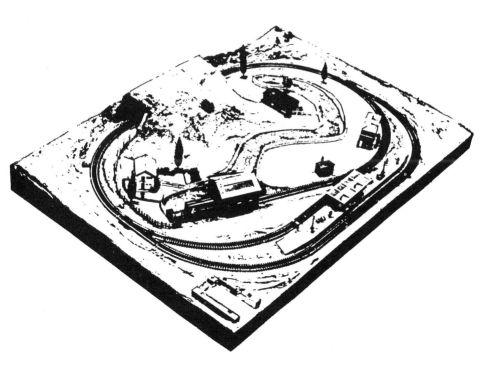

4

Introduction

The construction of a model railway layout can give the builder a great deal of enjoyment and satisfaction, but this is by no means all that the hobby has to offer. Operation of the completed layout in a realistic manner, following the principles of real railway practice, can provide continuing interest and entertainment for the enthusiast and his or her friends. Many modellers never realise the full potential of this aspect of the hobby and their running is merely haphazard. My aim in this book is to show the beginner how even a small and simple model railway can be operated in an interesting and realistic manner. There are various methods of running a model railway and we will look at the basic principles of some of these so that you can choose the one most suitable for you and your layout.

If the modeller is to gain the maximum pleasure from operating his layout it is essential that the model railway should run smoothly and reliably. For a layout to operate properly regular maintenance and repairs are required. Many beginners are uncertain just how to go about keeping their layouts and equipment in good order, and also feel that such work is likely to be a tedious chore anyway. However, for the most part, simple care and maintenance that you can easily carry out yourself is all that

is needed and I will cover these basic procedures in this book.

Participation in model railway exhibitions and shows can be a very enjoyable and satisfying activity for the enthusiast but also demands careful preparation for the most successful results. In the final section of this book I want to give the beginner some suggestions regarding this preparation and also about attendance and actual operation at the exhibitions themselves.

I would like to thank all those modellers who have kindly allowed me to use pictures of their models and layouts to illustrate this book. In particular I am grateful to Harold Bowcott, members of the Brooklands Railway Society Model Group, Allan Downes, members of the Greenwich & District Narrow Gauge Railway Group, Brian Monaghan, Bob Petch and Dick Wyatt. I am especially indebted to Chris Ellis for permission to include the description of how he compiled a timetable for his N-scale layout and to Geoff Barlow for his advice on maintenance and repairs. I am also grateful to those manufacturers who have provided information and pictures of their products, and particularly to Matt Ascough of M & R (Model Railways) Ltd for his assistance with information on the Fleischmann hump yard.

Left *Modern railway operation is a complex business but is built up from many simple train movements. In the same way model railway operation should be kept simple at first and developed later as experience is gained.*

The train set

The gift or purchase of a train set is the introduction to railway modelling for many enthusiasts and it is probably a good place for us to begin in considering model railway operation. With the basic train set oval the scope for operation is very limited indeed. We can run a train clockwise or anti-clockwise around the oval, we can stop it, start it and reverse it, and that is about all. Even if we place a station or two on the oval and use our imagination to pretend the train is running, say from London to Newcastle, with stops at various stations en route, the layout will not be very interesting to run. No matter how realistic the structures and scenery providing the setting for the railway are, the modeller will soon tire of the layout.

The operational interest and variety will be considerably increased by the addition of even two or three sidings as then we can carry out shunting duties. Trailing sidings are easily worked. The train stops short of the points and it is divided immediately behind the wagon or wagons intended for the siding. The engine and front part of the train then pulls forward over the points, these are changed and the train reverses on to the siding. The wagon or wagons for the siding are uncoupled and left there as the engine moves out of the siding on to the main line. The points are changed again and the engine backs up to reform the train. For a siding served by a facing point it is more difficult. The train stops short of the siding and is split immediately in front of the wagon or wagons for the siding. The engine must then run right round the oval to reach the rear of the train. The siding point is changed and the locomotive then pushes the train on to the siding. The wagon or wagons for the siding are uncoupled and left there while the engine pulls the remainder of the train out of the siding on to the main line again. The point is changed and the locomotive must again run right round the oval, this time to reach the front of the train once more. Normally when a train is made up, wagons destined for the same siding will be placed together but, if for any reason they have not been, then further moves will be required to sort them out at the siding. Similarly, if there are one or more wagons to be collected by the train from the siding this will add to the movements needed as they must be removed

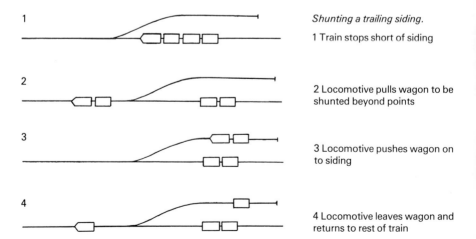

Shunting a trailing siding.

1 Train stops short of siding

2 Locomotive pulls wagon to be shunted beyond points

3 Locomotive pushes wagon on to siding

4 Locomotive leaves wagon and returns to rest of train

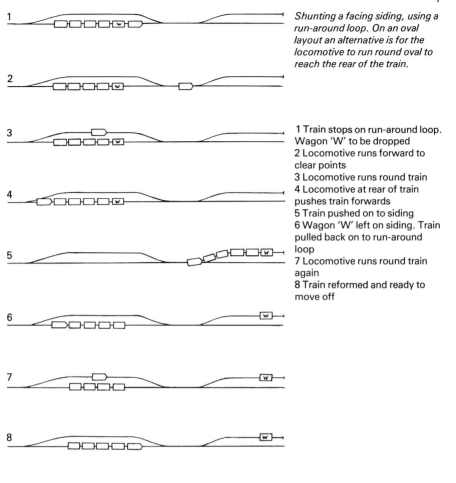

Shunting a facing siding, using a run-around loop. On an oval layout an alternative is for the locomotive to run round oval to reach the rear of the train.

1 Train stops on run-around loop. Wagon 'W' to be dropped
2 Locomotive runs forward to clear points
3 Locomotive runs round train
4 Locomotive at rear of train pushes train forwards
5 Train pushed on to siding
6 Wagon 'W' left on siding. Train pulled back on to run-around loop
7 Locomotive runs round train again
8 Train reformed and ready to move off

Placing two industries on one siding adds to the traffic and to the number of moves required in shunting. To shunt vans to warehouse, wagons at factory must be removed then replaced.

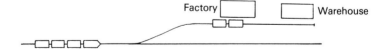

Factory   Warehouse

A kick-back siding also increases the shunting moves needed. To shunt wagons on to kick-back siding serving factory warehouse, siding must first be cleared.

Factory   Warehouse

The train set

Above *The addition of a run-around loop and a siding to the basic oval makes it possible to run two trains on the layout, though not simultaneously, and to carry out a little shunting, as on this small simple layout built by Terry Jenkins.* **Below** *Here a Mainline 0-6-0 Tank Engine shunts the goods siding on Terry Jenkins' small layout.* **Right** *If a run-around loop is added to the basic train set oval the engine can reach the rear of the train for reversing direction. It also makes the shunting of facing sidings more convenient.*

from the siding before the arriving wagons are shunted on to the track. Further complications arise if one siding serves two different facilities or industries. In this case a wagon at the nearer one may have to be temporarily removed to allow access to a wagon further along the siding, and then replaced in position at the conclusion of the shunting. If there is a fan of sidings, a set of two or more sidings from a single lead from the main line, then there is additional scope for sorting of the arriving wagons. We can provide various facilities, a goods shed, a cattle dock, coal staithes and so on, for these sidings, adding to the interest and the appearance. A kick-back siding is a track leading off, in the reverse direction, from another siding. Because the main siding must be cleared to allow the locomotive to shunt the kick-back siding such an arrangement adds to the number of shunting movements required. Some modellers find this a nuisance and hence do not bother to shunt the kick-back siding. However, if you like shunting, and particularly if your layout is small and thus needs as much operating potential as possible in what space is available, you may benefit from including one or more sidings of this type on it. An advantage of such sidings is that they enable you to place extra tracks in situations where the space could not otherwise be utilised for sidings.

With a simple oval layout with sidings it is possible to accommodate two trains, one on the main line and the other stored on a siding, though they cannot both be run at the same time. The provision of a run-around or passing loop will make shunting more convenient and will add to the operational flexibility. To reverse the train it is stopped on one track of the loop, clear of both points, and the locomotive is uncoupled and run ahead to clear the points. It is then moved back along the other track past the train and over the points behind the train. The engine is then advanced to be coupled to the rear of the train. If it is a goods train with a guards van to be transferred as well as the engine, then additional moves will be required. Similarly, when shunting a siding served by a facing point the locomotive can run round the loop to reach the rear of the train and does not need to travel right round the oval. A passing loop also makes it more convenient to operate two trains on a small oval layout, as one can be held on one track of the loop while the other travels around the main line, using the other track of the passing loop to go by the stationary train. When desired the moving train can be stopped on the loop track and the other train can be run on the main line. Again, only one train can be in action at once.

On a point to point layout the provision of a

The train set

passing loop at an intermediate station will allow trains running in opposite directions to pass at the station, and will also facilitate shunting. At a small terminus a run-around loop is almost always provided so that the locomotive of an arriving train can move round to the other end of the train for the return journey. The presence of the loop also means that both facing and trailing sidings can be shunted. Often the loop is made up by including a release crossover between two tracks and the loop is frequently positioned alongside the platform or platforms saving space on the layout. However, it can alternatively be placed before the platform where it may be more convenient for goods trains, which usually share the same run-around loop at small stations. In this case, the passenger trains will be reversed on to the loop after arrival for the engine to run round and then return to the platform to await departure.

With this arrangement it is easy, if you wish, to provide separate arrival and departure tracks and platforms. Push-pull or auto-trains, railcars and multiple units do not, of course, require a run-around loop as they can operate equally well in either direction. Occasionally at small termini, and often on the platform roads at larger termini, no release crossover is provided. In this situation the arriving train, after the passengers have left, is uncoupled from the locomotive and is then pulled away to the carriage sidings by another engine, often the station pilot. Once the coaches have been removed the original train locomotive moves away to the engine servicing area. Except at small stations a head shunt is usually provided. This is a track parallel to the main line and linked to the sidings so that a locomotive can shunt the goods sidings without the need to use the main line; thus the latter is left clear for trains arriving at and departing from the station.

If we have double track on our oval or point to point line then it becomes easy to run two trains simultaneously, but in many ways operation is more interesting with the difficulties imposed by using single track with passing loops. The need to time train movements correctly so that the trains can pass each other at the loops with the minimum of delay will add to the interest. Thus, even with a simple layout built up from a train set we can carry out most of the basic train movements. Though many of these are straightforward the beginner does need to familiarise himself with the correct methods. He will also find that, with practice, he will become more adept and efficient, both at carrying out the actual movements and also at planning his shunting so that the minimum number of moves will be required. He will also become skilled at running his locomotives smoothly and at a realistic speed while shunting.

These moves, though an essential part of running a model railway, are the 'how' rather than the 'why' of operation. Having considered some of the details of train movements we can now look at the aims of operation.

Aims and advantages of operation

For some modellers the great interest in the hobby comes from the construction. They may enjoy all types of this work or may tend to specialise in one or more aspects, for example, trackwork, scenery or locomotives. For them the enjoyment comes with building the layout and, in many cases, once the work is essentially completed, they lose much of their enthusiasm. They may run a few trains in a rather haphazard manner, but are soon planning extensions, alterations or even a new layout. Now, of course, railway modelling is a hobby and it is up to the individual how he wishes to enjoy it. Indeed, one of the great advantages of this hobby is the very wide range of different activities which it offers. However, I do feel that many beginners who successfully construct layouts with much enjoyment and entertainment in the process are then rather uncertain of what to do with the completed model. They run trains in a random manner, in train set fashion, but are unaware of the great potential for entertainment that model railway operation can offer. Indeed, for some enthusiasts, construction of a layout, though satisfying in itself, is really just a means to an end — the operation of the layout. These modellers have created a fascinating form of game, with the entertainment value of a complex board game, but with the added attraction of seeing authentic models in action in a realistic scenic setting. One of the American pioneers in model railway operation, the late Frank Ellison, likened the operation of a layout to the presentation of a play in a theatre and certainly the running of some of the large and complex model railroads in the United States, by teams of skilled operators, can be a dramatic and exciting performance.

Already we have seen that, even on a small oval layout of the type easily developed from a train set, running a train, especially a goods train, can involve us in a considerable number of train movements. However, interesting though they can be, the movements I have described are really only the mechanics of how we handle the train once we have decided when and where that train will run.

For operation which will remain interesting and entertaining on a model railway layout, we must base it as realistically as possible on the way in which prototype railways are run. The aim of the real railways is to transport people and goods as efficiently and economically as possible, within the limitations imposed by safety regulations and any commitments with regard to services they are obliged to provide, even though they may be unprofitable. Obviously there are limitations, particularly due to lack of space, on our layouts but, as far as possible, our trains should reproduce the operation of the real ones. Thus our trains should appear to have a purpose when they move and not just look as if they are running haphazardly, as the whim of the operator takes them. On the prototype, goods vehicles are moved according to the needs of the customers and we must be sure that we distribute our rolling stock in a realistic manner representing the transport of goods between customers.

Thus what we require is some system or scheme of operating which will give the impression that our trains are travelling around the layout in the same way as prototype trains on the real railways. Generally, the best results will come from using a system based on or adapted from prototype operation. Because of this some familiarity with prototype practice is beneficial and, indeed, finding out more about how the real thing runs can be very interesting in itself as well as helping you to operate your own layout more realistically.

Various methods have been devised by different modellers to suit their own layouts and the type of operation which interests them most. The majority of these schemes are based either on timetable, or sequence, operation, on some system of rolling stock distribution, or on a combination of both. Later in this book we will look at some of the possibilities that you could employ on your model railway.

Now you may be thinking that the idea of prototype-based operation and the use of a timetable is all very well on a large and complex

A small branch line terminus beautifully modelled in 4 mm scale by Allan Downes. All the structures were scratch-built. Such a station provides a good introduction to model railway operation but the scope is somewhat limited as prototype branch lines usually run rather restricted timetables. (Photograph by Brian Monaghan.)

layout with several operators, but that it is not relevant for a small and simple one-man model railway. However, this is not so and, even on a small oval layout, such as might be developed from a train set, it is perfectly feasible to run a timetable or sequence operation scheme. Admittedly, some imagination is required. For example, the journey is often made up of a number of laps of the circuit and we must ignore the fact that the train keeps passing the same features on each lap of the track. However, a model railway can never be an exact replica of the real thing so we must always use some imagination; indeed it is part of the fun to do so. An example of how interesting operation can be provided by a

minimum space layout is given by a 3 feet by 2 feet N-gauge layout recently built by Chris Ellis. Despite the small size and simple track plan, a realistic and entertaining schedule has been devised. In a later section in this book Chris Ellis explains how he drew up the timetable and the reasoning behind it.

It was the search for greater realism in railway modelling despite limited space and other resources that encouraged the development of the concept of branch line modelling. Because the branch line model railway forms a good introduction to operation, and in fact to scale railway modelling in general, I would like to consider the subject in more detail.

Branch line operation

If we are to have a realistic model railway in a small space with a necessarily simple track plan we must select a suitable prototype—the country branch line in the days of steam is an ideal choice. Trains often consisted of only two or three coaches or a few wagons pulled by a small tank engine and the station track layouts were usually fairly simple.

During the 1950s the branch line model railway concept was developed considerably. At that time the idea was not so much to provide a suitable subject for beginners as to enable more experienced workers to create a model railway which was realistic in appearance and operation in a small space. The short prototype trains allowed the modeller to run authentic length trains despite the small size of the layout. Also, because the station track layouts were simple on branch lines, they can be compressed to fit on to a model railway while still keeping their essential features. Thus the model can be operated according to prototype practice and following a proper timetable.

The aim was not to make an exact scale model of a particular branch line station; even the simple stations on country branches occupied a considerable ground area and would take too much space on a layout if reproduced accurately to scale. If space for this was available it would be better utilised in modelling a more complex and more interesting station with greater operating potential. In fact, though some enthusiasts have been very successful in basing their branch line stations closely on particular prototypes, many modellers find that it suits them better to combine features from a variety of real stations to produce an interesting and attractive model with all the features they want.

To reiterate then, the key points are having realistic trains operating in an authentic manner. The advantage of branch line stations is that their simple track plans, with few points, permit considerable selective compression without affecting the essential features which influence the way the station can be operated.

Because the aim was realistic operation, the point to point track arrangement was usually preferred to the continuous run schemes, and the now classic branch line terminus to fiddle yard (hidden sidings representing the rest of the system) design was developed. Such a track plan can be fitted on to baseboards of various shapes but a popular arrangement is on two narrow baseboards in an L shape, often fitted into the corner of a room. This design has the advantage of providing the greatest running possibilities in a minimum area and often a layout of this shape can be fitted into a room whereas a conventional rectangular baseboard would not be acceptable as it would block the centre of the room too much.

A branch line layout of this type is also very

A branch line layout can be the ideal intro-duction to model railway operation for the beginner.

Branch line operation

Above *Bob Petch's 00-gauge layout features a GWR branch line through station, Limpley, with a fiddle yard at each end of the line to complete the layout. Here a milk train has been held in the loop at the station to allow a mineral train to pass. Modelling a through station enables the operator to run traffic on the line for which there are no facilities at the station, giving greater scope than with a terminus. This photograph was taken at an exhibition; note the chairs at top right employed to keep the viewers clear of the model.*

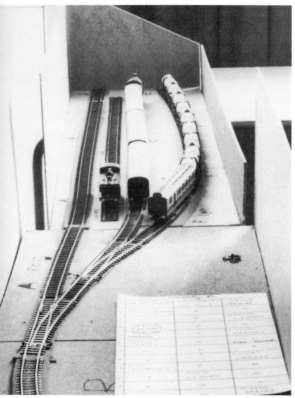

Left *One of the two fiddle yards on Bob Petch's layout. Note the sheet of instructions for the fiddle yard operator at bottom right of the picture.*

suitable for the beginner. Now that so many high quality ready-made items such as track, locomotives and rolling stock are available at very reasonable prices such a layout can quickly be brought to a stage where it is interesting to view and operate. The good quality of the commercial items means that, with reasonable care, even the beginner should achieve satisfactory running and be able to enjoy organised operation. It is also easy to add structures and scenery to give an attractive appearance.

The terminus to fiddle yard scheme lends itself very well to authentic operation, based either on a prototype timetable or on one devised by the modeller to suit his own stock and interests. Prototype branch line timetables were usually simple and were often operated on the 'one engine in steam' principle so there is no reason why the beginner with only one locomotive and a limited selection of rolling stock should not be able to run his layout in a realistic manner. The fiddle yard represents the rest of the branch and the junction station. Here trains are made up by hand, without worrying about any pretence of realism and are then despatched to the terminus station where any necessary shunting or other train movements are carried out in an authentic and realistic manner. The train then returns to the fiddle yard. The terminus can operate realistically following the timetable and dealing with all the trains from the imaginary junction.

Such a line is an excellent introduction to operation for the newcomer as it will get him started without difficulty. As he gains experience and additional rolling stock he can extend the basic timetable to make it more fun to operate. The disadvantage is that traffic on a prototype branch line was rather limited in scope and extent and, if the model is to be realistic, operation on it must necessarily also be relatively restricted. Running too intensive a service on a model branch line will destroy the illusion of realism which we are trying to create. Because of these limitations the modeller is likely to find that, in time, he loses interest and will then need to extend the layout or even scrap it and change to a larger system.

Though the classic terminus to fiddle yard scheme described above is the most popular design, there is an interesting alternative arrangement which was, I believe, first employed by Maurice Deane. This is to fit the branch line on a rectangular baseboard with a central operating well and with the line curved round so that the fiddle yard is behind the terminus, concealed by a low backscene. This has the advantage that the modeller working alone can easily reach both the terminus and the fiddle yard beyond it from his operating position in the central well. It also makes it easy to include a link to create an oval so that continuous running is possible if desired. The link can be concealed so that the realism of the point to point scheme is not impaired.

Another idea in which there has been more interest recently, perhaps partly to provide a change from the usual design, is the modelling of a through station on a branch line rather than the terminus. Such an arrangement can be operated as an oval with hidden sidings on the side opposite to the through station, or as a point to point design with a fiddle yard at each end, a reversing loop at each end or with a fiddle yard at one end and a reversing loop at the other, making up an out and back arrangement. The choice of a through station does have certain advantages, particularly in allowing greater scope for traffic on the line.

Branch line operation

Traffic on your railway

Before we can plan a timetable or schedule for a layout we must have some idea of the traffic it should carry. The prototype railways, of course, must cope with whatever traffic they are offered. Passengers wish to travel from town to town, commercial and industrial customers want goods and freight transferred to and from their factories, warehouses and depots, and so on. Trains are run to handle these demands and the make up of these trains may be adjusted from day to day and from season to season according to variations in the traffic.

Now if we are modelling a specific station or are basing our layout on a particular line, more or less closely, then the type of traffic will largely be determined for us. From the working timetable of the prototype, if it is available, from details about the line in books and magazine articles, and from a knowledge of the nature of the countryside served by the railway, we can build up an accurate picture of the traffic the line would carry. If we have, on the other hand, created our own station and line we must also develop a background for it. We may choose to base it on a particular area and we can then follow the general traffic trends for lines in the part of the country concerned. Alternatively, we may wish to create our own imaginary countryside for the railway to run through.

Whatever course we choose, it is important to build up a background picture of this sort if we are to have a realistic pattern of traffic for the layout. The branch line again serves as a useful example, partly because it is a good subject for a beginner's first scale layout, and partly because the simple timetable of the prototype makes a good introduction to model railway operation. Let us consider the small branch line terminus first of all. It is likely to be in a country area or serving a small coastal port or seaside town. If we model a terminus station then traffic on our layout from the fiddle yard to the terminus must stop there. All movements on the layout should have a purpose, if our operating is to appear realistic, so wagons will only be moved from the fiddle yard to the terminus and back if there is freight to be carried to or from the station. As the station is a terminus, the type of rolling stock on the line will be limited by the traffic handling facilities at the station. For example, if we have no cattle dock then we cannot run cattle wagons, and so on. If you find this unduly limiting you may prefer to model a through station. This is much less restricting regarding the rolling stock we operate on the line as we can always say that stock for which there are no facilities at the station is merely en route to other destinations further along the line!

Coming back to our small terminus we can first of all consider the passenger traffic. We will need a train early in the morning to take people from the small town to work at the junction town or at other places along the main line from there (all represented by the fiddle yard) and a train to bring them back in the late afternoon or early evening. A train going later in the morning and one back during the afternoon will provide a service for shoppers while a train each way in the evening will cope with passengers wanting to spend an evening at the cinema or at other entertainments in the

Top right *This wooden extension to the platform was provided for milk traffic at Watlington and has been faithfully reproduced on the Mid Hants Model Railway Group model of the station.* **Above right** *The Mid Hants Model Railway Group's accurate model of Watlington station, an Oxfordshire branch line terminus, in EM gauge. This picture shows part of the goods yard which has facilities typical of a small country station. The beautifully detailed goods shed was scratch-built by Barry Fisher. The track on the right is used for coal wagons and storage.* **Right** *Typical traffic at a country branch line station includes livestock and farm equipment as seen here on the EM-gauge model of Watlington station. Note the many small details which add interest and realism to the scene.*

Traffic on your railway

Above *A Hornby 0-6-0 Pannier Tank Engine and an auto-coach made up from a BSL kit form this typical auto-train seen at Stonepark Lane, an 00-gauge country branch line terminus. Because these trains run in either direction the engine does not need to run round the train at the terminus.* **Above right** *Livestock was an important part of the goods traffic on many branch lines and the pens at Corfe Castle station on the 00-gauge model of the Swanage branch, built by the Isle of Purbeck Model Railway Club, contain cattle, sheep and pigs.* **Right** *The provision of industrial sidings will add greatly to the scope and interest of operation. On Harold Bowcott's 00-gauge layout, sidings serve this large factory and the hopper for the transfer of minerals from the narrow-gauge line at the left of the picture.* (Photograph by Brian Monaghan.)

larger town. Some of these services can be by push-pull train or a railcar but these involve less movements as no running round by the engine is required. Therefore it is best to have some of the services provided by ordinary trains so that there will be more shunting. Extra trains will be needed on Saturdays and on market days. If we place our terminus at a seaside or holiday resort then we will need more trains in the summer and may run through coaches or even through trains from London or other cities for the holiday visitors. In rural areas we may need additional trains for seasonal workers depending on the crops grown in the district. Thus variety can be introduced in the passenger traffic for even a fairly small terminus.

When we look at the freight side there is even more scope. Domestic coal was an important item in the days of the steam-operated branch line and our station should have a siding with coal staithes for this traffic. In addition, if we base a locomotive at the

terminus with a small engine shed and water tower we will need to provide coal for it and this will make up extra coal traffic on the line.

In a rural area much of the freight traffic will be related to agriculture. This may be crops, grain, vegetables or fruit which will need to be shipped out. Incoming traffic will include fertilisers and occasionally farm equipment such as a plough or tractor. The area may be more concerned with livestock so that we need to provide a cattle dock or sheep pens at our terminus, together with appropriate rolling stock to transport the animals. If horses are to be carried we will need one or more horse boxes on our rolling stock roster. Animal feed shipped in will further add to the traffic. There will also be goods coming in for the shops and the local pub, together with items ordered by people living in the town or village and on nearby farms.

If we have room for a dairy, a small sawmill or a quarry we can introduce suitable extra rolling stock to handle this special traffic; the

additional operational scope will also increase the interest. However, we should not run any stock for which there is clearly no traffic being generated if we are to maintain the realism. If we have chosen a small port as the setting for our terminus we can introduce fish traffic with a special fish train running through to the junction or beyond. There may also be goods brought to the dock for shipment in coastal freighters.

We may have space for a larger station and this will enable us to include more facilities and to introduce more types of traffic, making both the selection of rolling stock and the scope of operation more interesting. The terminus would be serving a larger town and we can probably provide some light industry. This will require incoming raw materials and perhaps coal as fuel, and there will be finished goods to be shipped out.

No hard and fast rules need be laid down regarding the traffic. The important thing is for there to be visible facilities and reasons for the traffic and that it should be appropriate to the area and to the type of community that your station serves. It is useful to decide on this sort of background to your line before planning the traffic and timetable so that you are quite clear just what your aims are. Otherwise you may be tempted to add this and that and to acquire unsuitable rolling stock, resulting in an unrealistic overall effect.

The whole concept can be approached in

Traffic on your railway

Above *Motorail services are now widely available in Britain and Europe. These two pictures show the facility at Narbonne on the SNCF. Special services of this type can be an interesting addition to model railway operation.* **Below** *Such services are often not exclusive to the contemporary scene. Here we see 'Motorail' Victorian style modelled on Mike Sharman's 4 mm scale period layout!*

various ways. One method is to decide on the location and type of line and to build up a picture of the sort of traffic pattern the railway should have. The layout can then be designed to fit in with this. Alternatively you can start with an already completed layout plan, perhaps a published design, and then plan out from this a traffic pattern which would be appropriate for the facilities provided. If you work from a prototype track plan, such as often appear in magazines and books, you can carry out a similar exercise but you will also have additional information available about the line and the area in which it was situated to help create a realistic and authentic operating scheme.

Once we have decided on the sort of traffic our line will carry we will have a good idea of the type of trains we will be running and of the rolling stock required. For the amount of traffic, most modellers use prototype lines of a similar nature as a guide or, if they are copying a particular prototype, they follow the pattern of that line. Often country branch lines had very simple timetables with relatively few trains, and modellers may wish to introduce a little more activity with a few extra trains, though this must not be overdone or the character of the model will be distorted. Even if your station serves an imaginary town you can work out the amount of traffic which would be likely by using real towns of a similar size as a guide. For example, David Jenkinson calculated the daily wagon movements for cattle, coal, minerals, milk and general goods stock on his Marthwaite layout using statistics from Settle and Carlisle stations as a basis. His excellent description appeared in the December 1966 issue of *Railway Modeller* magazine and gives a good example of how the traffic pattern for a model railway layout can be logically built up to give a realistic and authentic operating scheme.

Once we have a clear idea of the traffic our line will carry, we can go on to produce a schedule or timetable setting out the details of how our trains will run. Before devising a timetable for our layout it is perhaps a good time to look briefly at the real thing.

Traffic on your railway

Prototype timetables

The railway timetables with which everyone is familiar are the public timetables which cover only the passenger train schedules listing only their times for the stations at which they stop. Much more useful for the railway modeller interested in operation are the working timetables, issued to employees of the railway. These list all trains on the line concerned, passenger and freight, with their timings and with many other details such as train numbers and classification, speed restrictions, information regarding stops for shunting, for other trains to pass, and so on. These timetables are private and not for publication or general distribution. However, many are available unofficially in railway enthusiast circles

and a number, mainly from steam days, have been published. For example, The Oxford Railway Publishing Company Ltd can offer Cambrian Railway (1904), Somerset & Dorset Railway (1920), Southern Railway (West Division) (1932) and Southern Railway (Isle of Wight) (1932) Passenger and Working Timetables, and more timetable reprints are to be published in due course. Many books on particular branch lines include details of their working timetables and these are invaluable to modellers building layouts based on these lines. The excellent books *Great Western Branch Line Termini* Vols 1 & 2 by Paul Karau, published by The Oxford Railway Publishing Company, for example, include working timetables for the branches concerned and also very useful details on how the termini were operated. Even if you are not modelling one of these lines the timetables would be a useful guide if you are operating a branch line layout.

If the modeller has chosen a specific branch, either to model exactly or as a general basis for his layout and he can obtain the working timetable for the period he wishes to model then there will be no difficulty in running an accurate timetable service. As mentioned earlier familiarity with the economy of the area modelled and with the type of traffic the branch carried will enable him to realistically represent operation on the line. If it is not possible to find a copy of the authentic timetable it is still possible to devise a reasonable schedule from the track plan, station facilities and from what is known of the general type and extent of the traffic. Alternatively a timetable from a similar branch could be employed, perhaps with modifications to suit the needs of the modeller.

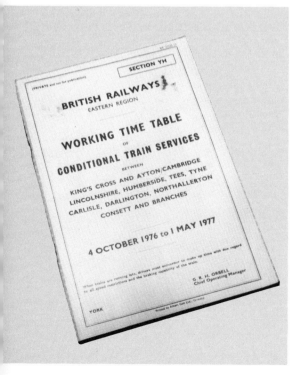

Left *Working timetables are issued to employees and give much more information than the ordinary public timetables, making them especially useful for railway modellers interested in operation.*

Compiling a simple timetable

Having considered the type of traffic we will have on our line, and perhaps with some prototype timetables to guide us, we can tackle the job of producing our first simple timetable. It is important not to try to devise anything too complicated at first as it is easy to become confused by too many details even though the principles may be straightforward. Because of its simplicity a branch line terminus timetable makes a good beginning. Again as branch line timetables were often very simple, frequently such lines operated on the one engine in steam principle, they can be conveniently carried out in model form using the sequence method. This type of running is well suited to the beginner to model railway operation and is also

especially suitable for one modeller operating on his own, as is often likely to be the case with a small branch line layout.

Sequence operation is a simple but orderly pattern of operation which overcomes the difficulty that, with a simple timetable (such as would apply to a small branch line terminus or through station) there will be long time intervals between trains. Because of this there are likely to be periods when the operator has nothing to do for some minutes, even when using a speeded-up clock system. With sequence operation a list of train movements is drawn up, as with an ordinary timetable, but these are carried out in simple sequence without regard to the time. Once one move-

A simple timetable.
SX = Except Sunday. **SO** = Sunday only. **Auto** = Auto Train. **Pass** = Passenger.

DOWN TRAINS	PASS	AUTO SO	AUTO SX	MIXED SX	AUTO SO	PASS	AUTO	AUTO
	am	am	am	am	pm	pm	pm	pm
FIDDLE YARD	7.30	9.40	9.55	11.30	1.06	5.10	6.30	8.35
HALT	7.38	9.48	10.03	11.46	1.14	5.18	6.38	8.48
TERMINUS	7.49	9.59	10.14	12.08	1.25	5.29	6.46	8.59

UP TRAINS	PASS	AUTO SO	AUTO SX	GOODS SX	AUTO SO	PASS	AUTO	AUTO
	am	am	am	pm	pm	pm	pm	pm
TERMINUS	8.02	10.20	10.30	1.04	1.35	5.40	7.00	9.05
HALT	8.13	10.31	10.41	1.26	1.46	5.51	7.11	9.16
FIDDLE YARD	8.21	10.41	10.49	1.42	1.54	5.59	7.19	9.24

Compiling a simple timetable

ment has taken place the operator goes on to the next. Thus it does not matter how quickly or slowly the enthusiast carries out the operations. If he wishes to pause he can do so, merely commencing again with the next train on the list. This is ideal for the beginner as he can get used to running the trains at realistic speeds and to carrying out shunting, also in a smooth and authentic manner, without being under any pressure to keep to time. And conversely there are no periods when he has nothing to do but wait. There is no reason why the modeller should not work through a prototype timetable using this system. Instead of sending out a train at, for example, 2.25 pm either by real or scale time, the train is despatched in its turn, and the time then is regarded as being 2.25 pm. Sequence operation, as I have mentioned previously, is particularly suited to operation of a simple layout, especially a branch line terminus or through station layout with one engine only running at any one time. Here there is not the need, as there may be on a larger more complex layout with two or more operators, for trains to pass or meet other trains or to clear trackage by a certain time. When there are more operators and there are trains which must interlock in their running we need some standard, most conveniently provided by all running to the same clock, whether speeded up or not, so that operation maintains an orderly pattern. Otherwise chaos may result.

As I have already indicated, sequence operation is particularly suitable for the single handed operator though it can still be used with two or more modellers. In this case they can all work from the same sequence card. Alternatively, they can work from cards of their own but provision must be made for keeping the sequence, either by exchanging cards between operators at the appropriate stages, or by including instructions that a particular movement must not be carried out until after the other operator has made some move.

Ideally at the end of the sequence all the stock should be back where it started so that the next sequence can begin. Generally, as with timetables, it is a good idea to begin with a simple limited sequence, then add to it as you gain experience and stock. If a particular sequence becomes boring after a time through repetition, then rearrange it to provide some variety. Extra interest can also be added by running some unscheduled trains such as a track repair train, a special passenger train, perhaps to bring people to an agricultural show, a seasonal goods train for a fruit crop, and so on.

To complete this section I would like to give you an example of how one modeller has created an interesting and realistic operating scheme for a very small layout. Chris Ellis recently built an N-gauge layout only 3 feet by 2 feet in size. He has described the construction of the layout in a series of articles in the magazine, *Model Train,* and I am most grateful for his permission to include here his working timetable and an outline, based on his description, of how he developed this timetable. His layout is based on an American prototype, the Chicago & North Western Railroad, but the basic principles are essentially similar to the making of a timetable for a British line.

The Warren, Beresford and Chicago Railroad was designed to provide interest in operation as well as in construction, and the operating concept of the layout was evolved as

Opposite and following three pages *Operation on the N-gauge American prototype Warren, Beresford and Chicago layout built by Chris Ellis.* (All photographs by Chris Ellis.) **1** *An operator using the timetable alongside the controller. A Scoot is in the fiddle yard, at the rear centre of the picture, ready to run to Warren.* **2** *The Scoot moving along the fiddle yard siding heading up the branch to Warren.* **3** *Switching at North Warren. The Illinois Central reefer (refrigerated car) is being pulled out of the dairy siding. It will be put on the 'main line' and the Lackawanna boxcar will replace it at the dairy loading bank. The tank car will then go on to the Shell siding.* **4** *The Lackawanna boxcar is now being spotted at the dairy.* **5** *The branch freight approaching Warren headed by the Fairbanks-Morse H-12-44 switcher (Minitrix model repainted in Chicago and North Western colours).* **6** *Scoot (Train No 914) heading for Chicago (pushing) while the local freight is switched at North Warren.* **7** *Local mine train (No 910) arrives in the fiddle yard and is removed from the track.* **8** *Switching is suspended while Scoot No 913 arrives at the station at Warren. The local freight locomotive has gone to North Warren to lay over.* **9** *The Scoot has departed and the local freight locomotive arrives back at Warren to resume switching, bringing with it the cars picked up at North Warren.* **10** *Local freight locomotive laying over at North Warren while the Scoot occupies Warren station (see photo 8).* **11** *Switching the mine — Train No 909 changing loaded hoppers for the empties it has just brought in. Note the flagman on the road crossing.* **12** *Train No 912 — the local freight returning from Warren/North Warren to Chrystal Lake.*

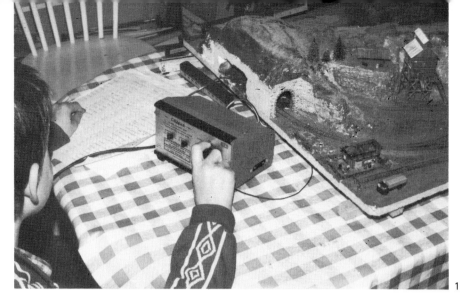

2

1

3

4

5

6

7

8

9

10

11

12

follows. First of all, think in basic terms. What is the aim of the railroad? The answer is to carry people and goods from one point to another. Our layout is the most basic form of railway, a simple single track branch line doing exactly that, carrying goods and people from an 'off-stage' location (the equivalent of the fiddle yard on the classic branch line terminus type of layout) to the stations and depots on the board. From here it is a matter of choosing a location for the line. You can make up a completely mythical line with a 'company' name of its own if desired. Or you can do as we did and find a suitable railway to which your 'branch' can be connected as a fictional addition. The further alternative of modelling an actual location was not really practical for a small oval layout like this because there is insufficient space to represent it properly.

This led us to a 'fictional addition' to a real railway. We wanted a railway which would lend itself to a simple compact branch line, offer a busy service in real life, and enable us to use ready-to-run N-scale items with a minimum of adaptation. One line (but by no means the only one) which fitted these requirements was the Chicago North Western Railroad which operates out of Chicago, west and north-west as its name implies. This may seem somewhat exotic to some readers, but it is colourful in its snappy green/yellow paint scheme, it has a wide selection of motive power, it is a relatively small, tightly managed company, and it has lots of very rural country branch lines, almost as though the old Great Western Railway was still running its 1948 network in this modern diesel age. All the locomotives and stock required to operate a CNW layout are readily available in current N-gauge production, even though a little repainting and adaptation may be necessary. Above all, it operates a commuter service into Chicago which runs further out into the country than any of the other lines in the area with commuter service. Its route to the furthest commuter outpost, the holiday and residential resort of Lake Geneva, Wisconsin, is 73 miles by rail from Chicago on a branch of great charm and beauty.

By American standards the commuter trains offer a very frequent service, and these trains operated by double-decker (or bi-level) cars are short. So a branch line similar to the Lake Geneva branch offered us a modern era setting, with short trains, which could be dovetailed neatly into the existing network. The sketch map of the CNW routes, over which a commuter service operates, is included here and our branch is added to it, running to Warren (and North Warren—freight only) from Chrystal Lake. This new branch lends itself so

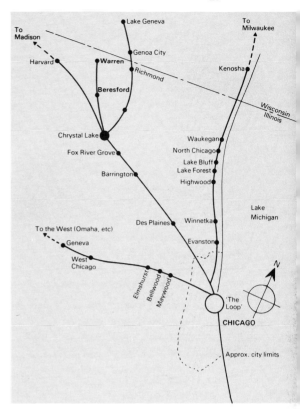

Sketch map showing the actual suburban routes from Chicago of the Chicago and North Western Railway system, with the addition of the fictional Warren branch coming off at Chrystal Lake. Only major stations are shown—there are actually more than 70 in the area of the map. Clybourn, mentioned on the train schedule, is the first junction out of Madison Street station in Chicago. (Courtesy Chris Ellis.)

well to existing CNW operations that we could readily produce a passenger schedule exactly like all other CNW leaflets you can pick up at stations on the line! If you do have access to a home printing set, it adds an amusing extra element to your layout if you have some realistic timetables to display and give to visitors.

A printed schedule, however, is really only the icing on the cake. It will impress your friends and help to bring the layout to life. To operate the layout with a logical schedule of runs you need something more mundane—a working timetable. Real timetables can appear very complicated and on a large model railway

Compiling a simple timetable

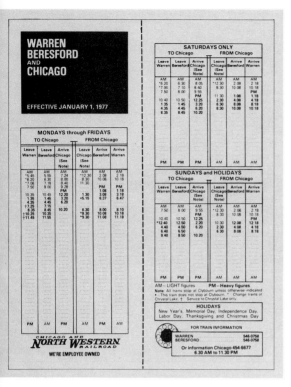

No.	Time (Warren)	From	To	Duty/Remarks
	WORKING TIMETABLE — WARREN			
901	2.18 am	C	W	Scoot — lays over at W
902	5.45 am	W	CL	Scoot — shuttle to CL and retu...
903	6.10 am	CL	W	Scoot — 902 returning to W
904	6.20 am	W	CL	Scoot — shuttle to CL and retu...
905	6.55 am	CL	W	Scoot — 904 returning to W
906	7.08 am	W	CL	Scoot — shuttle to CL and retu...
907	7.40 am	CL	W	Scoot 906 returning to W
908	7.50 am	W	C	Scoot — through to Chicago
909	8.15 am	CL	W	Mine train — work mine
910	8.45 am	W	CL	Mine train returning to CL
911	9.45 am	CL	W	Local freight from CL
912	As required	W	CL	Local freight returning to CL
913	10.18 am	C	W	Scoot — 8.30 from C
914	10.35 am	W	C	Scoot through to Chicago
915	As required	CL	W	Local freight from CL
916	As required	W	CL	Local freight to CL
917	1.18 pm	C	W	Scoot — 11.30 from C
918	1.35 pm	W	C	Scoot — through to Chicago
919	2.00 pm	CL	W	Mine train — work mine
920	2.30 pm	W	CL	Mine train — return to CL
921	3.18 pm	C	W	Scoot — 1.30 from C
922	4.35 pm	W	C	Scoot — through to Chicago
923	As required	CL	W	Local freight from CL
924	As required	W	CL	Local freight to CL
925	6.47 pm	C	W	Scoot — 5.15 from Chicago
926	7.05 pm	W	CL	Scoot — to Chrystal Lake
927	8.10 pm	C	W	Scoot — 6.30 from Chicago
928	8.35 pm	W	C	Scoot — through to Chicago
929	9.15 pm	CL	W	Mine train
930	9.45 pm	W	CL	Mine train — return to CL
931	10.18 pm	CL	W	Scoot — shuttle from CL (926 returning)
932	10.25 pm	W	CL	Scoot — shuttle to CL
933	11.18 pm	CL	W	Scoot (932 returning)
934	11.45 pm	W	CL	Scoot — to CL
901	2.18 am	CL	W	Scoot (934 returning) Lays over at W to form 902

Notes:
C = Chicago, Madison Street Station W = Warren CL = Chrystal L...
All times in column 2 are arrival/departure Warren

Left *The train schedule for the Warren, Beresford and Chicago layout was reproduced to the exact size and style of the real CNW passenger timetables.* (Courtesy Chris Ellis.) **Right** *Working timetable for the Warren, Beresford and Chicago layout.* (Courtesy Chris Ellis.)

operation can be complex. However, here we have only the simplest of single line branches on which it is physically impossible to run more than one train at a time. Consequently, our timetable should be a simple one.

For a start, we forgot about time, real or speeded up, since ours is a layout for leisurely home operation and the pace of working is entirely up to you. Yes, there are nominated arrival and departure times for all the trains operating in a sequence throughout the day, but these times are descriptive rather than actual. Looking at the working timetable given here you will see that the first train in the 24 hour weekday schedule is the 2.18 am arrival in Warren from Chrystal Lake—representing the connecting train (at Chrystal Lake) with the last train of the day out of Chicago. So if you choose to start an operating session with this train it is simply the 2.18 am, no matter what time your operating session starts.

Obviously, to work this out we had to know some basic timings and make some assumptions. So to start with we got hold of the train schedules for all the commuter runs on the CNW network. Using the train schedule for the Chicago-Harvard route (on which line is the all-important Chrystal Lake junction) it is easy enough to plot the frequency of passenger trains to and from the CNW station in Chicago. We made an early assumption here which was dictated by the limited trackage at Warren; because there are no spare sidings at Warren we could not have passenger trains 'laying over' waiting for their next turn, except for the last train at night which could lay over to become the first train in the morning. On the real railway, where most commuter runs are crowded into the morning or evening rush hours, the trains lay over in sidings in Chicago, Harvard, Chrystal Lake, etc, until they are next required for service. At Warren any such lay over would impede the running of freight trains, so incoming passenger trains are marked on the working timetable as returning to Chrystal Lake to lay over. A more likely alternative to this would be a siding 'off the board' beyond Beresford, where the train could be held until it returned to Warren for the next scheduled run to Chicago. At present this does not worry us—the train just runs back to siding A and is taken off the track until next required. If and when we extend the layout on to another board, we will worry about the actual destination then.

The other point peculiar to the CNW operation is that all trains are made up of bi-level (double-deck) cars and are push-pull operated using F7 or E8 diesel locomotives. So there is no need for the locomotive to run around the train at Warren. On the actual CNW commuter routes there may be anything from two to six passenger cars, the outer one a driving unit, depending on the density of the route. A single car is not usual, but may be seen on late or holiday workings on some routes. For the compact Warren branch we decided that a single trailer would be used for early and late trains running to Chrystal Lake only and two trailers would be used for trains running 'through' to Chicago. This is actually a happy assumption. As Chrystal Lake is on the Harvard-Chicago route, itself a main line, with a very frequent commuter train service, we reasoned that trains coming off the Warren branch would not be likely to duplicate runs to Chicago on an already busy main line. So we make only the most important trains run 'through' to Chicago and for the rest the passengers boarding at Warren and Beresford change at Chrystal Lake to a train already running on the Harvard-Chicago route.

Having placed all the key passenger train times at what is roughly the correct timing by real CNW standards, we could then pencil in all the freight train timings on the branch. It is most unlikely there would ever be 'through' freight workings on a small branch like this. So we assume that all freight cars for on-line customers or facilities are dropped or picked-up overnight by main line freight trains at the Chrystal Lake interchange sidings, then brought up the branch by a small locomotive assigned to the branch. In practice this is a Minitrix Fairbanks-Morse H-12-44 or an Atlas GP9.

It so happens that the timings we have invented dove-tail quite neatly with the passenger trains, but the assumption must be made from the timings that some of the freight trains must go into passing loops or sidings down the branch to let passenger trains through. We also ignored for the present that somewhere along the 18 miles of track between Warren and Chrystal Lake there may be other on-line industries with traffic to

exchange and so make further complications. At present, therefore, all the freight cars which arrive at Warren are for sidings 'on the board', not off it.

Of particular interest is the complication with the 9.45 am local freight. Long before it can finish its work at Warren and North Warren, the 10.18 am passenger train is due. So the freight locomotive has to clear the station tracks and in practice it goes round to North Warren and the train crew take a coffee break until the passenger train has departed again as the 10.35 am.

Following the American style, we have given each train working a number, odd numbers out from Chicago and Chrystal Lake, even numbers inbound. The prefix '9' is supposed to indicate the line or branch—in this case the Warren branch. Actually this reference number is much easier to follow and remember than the time of the train and in practice the number is used rather than the time. Thus the 9.45 am referred to above is called Train No 911 when we are operating. A full weekday schedule has no less than 34 workings—17 in each direction, and it takes a very full evening operating session to get through it all. Sometimes, in fact, we do not complete it, but the beauty of the system is that you can start and stop when and how you please. If you have only a spare half hour, run as many trains as you have time for, mark your progress on the timetable (tick off each working with a pencil when completed) and carry on from where you left off when you next get time for an operating session. In CNW parlance the push-pull commuter trains are known as 'Scoots' (because they scoot along

Track plan of the Warren, Beresford and Chicago N-gauge layout built by Chris Ellis. **1** *Beresford Station;* **2** *Oil depot;* **3** *Dairy;* **4** *Corn and feed elevator;* **5** *Farm machinery and produce merchant;* **6** *Mine;* **7** *Freight depot;* **8** *Warehouse;* **9** *Warren Station;* **10** *North Warren;* **A** *fiddle siding. Each square measures 12 in. (Courtesy Chris Ellis.)*

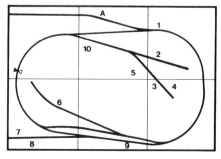

Compiling a simple timetable

32

quite fast!), and to save time on the timetable we have marked all passenger trains as 'scoots'. The working timetable reproduced here should be self-explanatory.

Do not be put off in any way by the fact that the trains and timetable on our actual layout are modern Chicago and North Western Railroad. You can run any trains that take your fancy on this type of layout without fundamentally changing the timetable. You can, of course, work out your own running sequence and times to suit yourself, but if you do not want to be bothered with this just photocopy our printed working timetable, change the station names and trains to suit your particular interest and away you go! With appropriate adaptations the line could be set in Wales, Scotland or Germany, the basic principles of the operation remain the same.

The other important point is that the layout and setting can equally well be in the steam or diesel age as you wish. Though our CNW 'scoots' are push-pull, there is no reason why the passenger trains should not be perfectly conventional with the locomotive running around the train for the return journey. We have done this ourselves by switching the diesel era of our layout over to steam on occasions, using the Minitrix Pennsylvania Railroad B6 0-6-0 and an 0-4-0 saddle tank. In this case the passenger train has been made up of a single 'steam age' PRR combine coach.

What we hope our timetable has shown is that even a very simple layout like this, little more than a development from a basic train set oval, still has massive operational potential far removed from merely running model trains round and round in circles. We found that when trying to work a full week-day timetable in an evening session there was not actually much time available for running trains round

and round but, if you want to make a few laps to simulate 'mileage' before bringing the train into the station, that is entirely up to you.

The above description by Chris Ellis clearly demonstrates that a simple sequence scheme of operation can create interesting and entertaining running on even a very small and simple layout, extending the enjoyment such a layout can give well beyond the period of construction. Such sequence operation is ideal for the beginner, new to the concept of model railway operation and still gaining skill in actually carrying out the various train movements. Indeed, many modellers find that the system suits them well and they continue to use it on their layouts without going on to anything more complicated. However, others feel that much of the interest, even excitement, in model railway operation comes from meeting the challenge of running to time, just as the real railways strive to do. It can be argued that as we have no real passengers on our model trains, and there is nobody sending out or waiting to receive the goods we pretend to be transporting on our railway, then we have no pressure to provide an efficient service unless we run to time. The protagonists of this argument feel that this is the best way to duplicate the operation of the real railways on a model layout. Certainly such operation can be an absorbing activity.

When introducing an operating system on a layout it is best to begin as a sequence scheme without the pressure of working to the clock. Later, as the operators become familiar with the system and gain experience generally, working to time can be added to the operating method. Basic to any system of operating to the clock is the matter of time and how we apply it to the model railway, and I would like to consider this subject next.

Time and the speeded-up clock

Now it can be argued that time is a constant factor and applies equally to models as to the real railway. And, indeed, if our model train is travelling at 60 scale miles per hour it will proceed a distance of 1 scale mile in 1 actual minute, just as the prototype at 60 miles per hour will travel 1 mile in the same actual time. So we could deduce that this is a logical argument and that we should run our timetable in accordance with an ordinary clock, and there are some modellers who do just that.

However, when we look a little further into the subject we find that there are definite disadvantages to this method. One very significant problem arises because of the short time it takes a train to run from one station to the next. Because it is usually quite impossible to model even a short branch line exactly to scale in the space we have for a layout, considerable compression is unavoidable in the model. This is selective, affecting particularly the length of track between stations. Thus, on most model railways the time taken for a train to travel between stations can be measured in seconds rather than minutes. Timetables both for the prototype and for model railways are made out to minutes, not seconds, so that these times between stations would have to be rounded up or down to the nearest minute and it is not possible to construct a satisfactory timetable on this basis. For example, if we have three stations, A, B and C on an 00-scale layout, with 10 feet of track from A to B and 20 feet from B to C, a train travelling at 20 scale miles per hour will take just under 30 seconds to go from A to B, which we must count as 0 minutes or 1 minute for our timetable. The time B to C will be just under 60 seconds, again counted as either 0 or 1 minute for the schedule. If the train travels at 40 scale miles per hour the times will be halved but must again be taken as either 0 or 1 minute for the timetable. Thus the use of standard time is quite inadequate for our purposes. If, however, we use fast time with a 12:1 ratio (5 minutes actual time becomes 1 hour fast time) the times A to B will become approximately 6 minutes

and 3 minutes respectively for 20 and 40 scale miles per hour, and similarly the times B to C will be about 12 minutes and 6 minutes. These enable us to compile a meaningful timetable.

There are many prototype operations that are unnecessarily long and it would be uninteresting on the model to allow the actual time they require. Another advantage of speeded-up time is that these functions will now take much less time. The use of fast time also makes it convenient to make small alterations in the schedules as found necessary by experience in running the layout. Say we have allowed 90 seconds for our train to pass between two points on the layout. If we use actual time this will be represented as either 1 or 2 minutes on the schedule. However, with 12:1 ratio speeded-up time this will be 18 minutes and, if necessary, we can adjust this to say 17 or 19 minutes, whereas with standard time we would still have to list it as 1 or 2 minutes.

Another reason for using speeded-up time is to retain the character of the operation of the real railways. To take an example, we can consider the intervals between trains, one following the other. On the prototype there may be an interval of 5 or 10 minutes and any delay of the first train will immediately affect the running of the second. On a model railway with an interval of 5 or 10 actual minutes the first train would have reached its destination long before the second train started, and the situation is not really representative of the operation on the prototype. With speeded-up time the actual interval on the model will be much less and the situation will be more like that on the real railway.

With many prototype timetables there are gaps in the schedule when there is no activity and these times can be boring interruptions to an operating session for which standard time is used. However, if we employ a speeded-up clock, these gaps will be very much shortened and will not be a significant interruption to the flow of operations.

Another benefit of the fast clock is that a full

Prototype railways impose speed restrictions which must be obeyed by drivers. This is a standard British Rail speed restriction sign, the numbers indicating the limit, here 30 miles per hour. The front faces of the numbers are yellow, the rest black.

24-hour timetable can be worked through in a single operating session. This means that the whole range of railway activity, day and night, can be enjoyed giving variety and hence extra interest to the session. It also has the advantage that, by working through the complete timetable at each session, the operators become familiar with it and, as they gain experience and skill, the running of the layout will be smoother and more enjoyable.

Having put forward a case for the use of fast time in model railway operation we must now consider just how fast this time should be. Some modellers assume that the ratio of fast to real time should relate to the scale in which they are working in some mathematically calculable way, but this is not so. A fundamental principal of the use of fast time in model railway operation is that there is no 'correct' scale time ratio for a particular scale; the ratio depends only on operating considerations. At first sight this may seem illogical but if we consider the situation in more detail we can

see that it is not basically the scaling down that introduces the need for fast time. As I mentioned in an example earlier, a model train will travel a scale mile at, say, 60 scale miles per hour in the same actual time, 1 minute, as a real train will take for a mile at 60 miles per hour. So, purely on the basis of scaling down, there is not necessarily any reason why we should not use standard time. It is the further compression of distances along the track, beyond that called for by scale, needed to fit a layout into a reasonable space that is a fundamental reason for using speeded-up time. We also find that many manoeuvres can be carried out more quickly on a model railway than on the prototype and this is a further reason for employing fast time.

This speeded-up time is often known as 'fast time'. Sometimes the term 'scale time' is used but, as this may be thought to imply some relationship to the scale of the model, it is perhaps not as good a term as 'fast time'. There have been attempts to justify the use of a particular relationship of this fast time to scale using various mathematical principles. For example, it has been suggested that we should apply Froude's equation, which is used to relate findings from the testing of models in wind tunnels and water tanks to the proto-types. Or that we should use the equation employed by movie makers when filming models to determine the appropriate camera speed so that, when screened at normal projection speed, the models in the film will move, and particularly fall, like the real thing. However, the idea of applying these principles to model railway operation is fallacious because, as explained above, the ratio depends not on the scale of the layout but on various operating considerations, though as it happens the results obtained do come within the range used by railway modellers.

Factors which do influence your choice include the distance between stations, train speeds and the efficiency of the operators at shunting and in carrying out other train move-ments of this type. It is also useful to choose a ratio which is convenient for measurementrs and calculations; the minimum interval of time should be a fast minute as we do not want to be involved with fractions of minutes in our schedule. The length of the 'day' on your railway, which may be 12 or 24 hours or some other period, and the average time you like an operating session to last may also influence your choice as there are advantages in being able to work through a full 'day' at a single session.

The ideal ratio depends to some extent on the type of operation on your railway. If it is

Operating your trains at scale speeds will improve the realism of your layout and you can impose appropriate scale speed limits. Suitable model signs are available from Smiths of Solihull and from R. Alderman of Yeovil. The 4 mm example shown here is from a Smiths set.

mainly running trains out on the line then, because of our greatly compressed distances, considerable speeding up of the time is desirable, especially if our stations are close together. On the other hand, if operation on our layout is largely shunting, perhaps on an industrial railway model, then the ratio should be smaller. One argument put forward against the use of fast time is that the discrepancy between the two types of operation will make it impossible to select a suitable ratio. These modellers claim that as shunting on the model will take much the same time as on the prototype, then using a speeded-up clock to make main line running more realistic will leave insufficient time for shunting to be carried out properly, or that inordinately long times will be needed on the timetable for shunting operations to be completed. In fact, two American modellers carefully timed shunting activities of various types on both prototypes and model railroads and found that, though it varies between different types of shunting, on

average such operations were still appreciably faster on the model. They were, incidentally, very careful that all model locomotive movements were carried out at scale speeds and in accordance with prototype practice. It is, therefore, quite feasible to find a compromise ratio which will improve operation on the main line and still permit realistic shunting.

The usual range of ratios of fast to standard time is somewhere between 6:1 and 15:1, with 12:1 perhaps the most popular, though 10:1 also has its advocates. The 12:1 ratio is convenient in that 5 minutes of standard time is equivalent to 1 hour of fast time, and a 24-hour day on the timetable can be worked through in a 2-hour operating session. The choice of ratio is up to the individual modeller and there is no reason why he should not adjust it later if he finds that it is set too high or too low for his layout. It has been suggested that a variable speed clock, or 'rubber' clock, is advantageous with inexperienced operators. If they fall behind schedule or are having difficulties of one sort or another then the clock can be slowed, or even stopped, until they catch up or sort out the problems. This has benefits when learning, both for training the operators and in deciding which will be the best ratio for your layout. However, once the operators have sufficient experience and the appropriate ratio has been selected it is best to try to stick to the proper timing and not to alter the clock. With

Time and the speeded-up clock

36

practice in working at a particular ratio, the operators become used to the fast time and familiar with the time needed for various manoeuvres and this is valuable in running the layout well. If the clock is being continually varied it takes much longer for this skill to be acquired.

Obviously, the most convenient method of working to fast time is to have a clock, or clocks, which have been adapted or altered in some way so that fast time can be read directly from it. Various modellers have modified clocks in different ways, usually by altering the gearing, so that they run faster. The details will vary with the particular clocks and with the degree of speeding-up required, and such alterations are beyond the scope of this book. I understand that digital clocks with integrated circuits can be altered by replacing the original time-base oscillator with one of higher frequency, or even with a variable frequency to produce a variable clock. Two articles have appeared in the American magazine, *Model Railroader,* one on altering an electric kitchen clock in the November 1955 issue, and one on modifying a digital clock in the November 1974 issue, and modellers wanting further information may like to refer to these articles.

A much simpler method is to use a clock without altering the mechanism but removing the hour hand and using the minute hand to read off the hours on a new face made up to suit the ratio selection. If you choose 12:1 you do not even need to make a new face, merely read off the hours as usual but with the minute hand. You can judge the intermediate times fairly well, especially if the spaces are marked out into minutes on the dial. If you are making a new clock face yourself you can divide the spaces between the hour marks into four quarters, each representing 15 minutes of fast time. Obviously reading a clock of this type will not be quite as accurate as one with the mechanism altered to speed it up but the times can still be judged sufficiently accurately for satisfactory operation.

To conclude our consideration of speeded-up time there is one final concept, that of the shortened mile, named the 'smile' by its originator, the late Frank Ellison, a pioneer of realistic model railroad operation. This measure is not related to scale but to the fast time ratio. A model train travelling at 60 scale miles per hour goes 1 scale mile in 1 minute of standard time; it also goes 1 'smile' in 1 fast minute. Thus the length of a 'smile' depends on the fast time ratio employed; for 10:1, for example, 1 'smile' = 0.1 scale mile. Though some modellers do install 'smile' posts at appropriate spacing on their main lines, 'smiles' do not really apply visually or in construction, but relate to timetable operation.

The train graph

Earlier we looked at a very simple timetable for a branch line with only one engine in steam. Here scheduling is very simple as there is only one train to be concerned with at any one time, running from the fiddle yard to the terminus and back. Because of the simplicity of the train movements, a mere list or table of the times is easy to compile and to interpret. On a more complex layout with perhaps two or three trains making journeys at the same time, and the need to arrange for trains to pass at specific places where there are passing loops, then a table of that type is much more difficult to compile and to understand. We need some other method which will enable us to determine more easily and quickly the relative positions and movements of the trains.

The simplest method is to follow the example of the prototype railways and make up a train graph on which the information is built up in an easy to understand visual form. It enables us to see, at a glance, where any train should be at any time and where and when it will pass other trains. These graphs, by convention, are laid out with the distance on the vertical axis. For the modeller this can be in scale miles, in actual feet, or if using fast time, in 'smiles'. It is useful to include a schematic track diagram along this axis also, together with the station names appropriately positioned. This is set out along the horizontal axis of the graph, either actual time or fast time, depending on the system you use on your layout. On such a graph the slope of the time lines is related to their speeds. When a train is stopped the train line will be horizontal, that is, though time passes, the distance does not change. The operators can work from train graphs or timetables can be compiled from the graph for running purposes. If you plan to work from the train graph it is convenient to make photocopies of the original graph for the

Each division is a short mile (smile)

An example of a train graph.

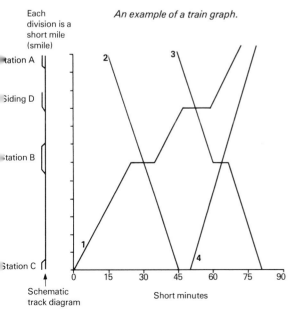

If vertical axis scale miles instead of 'smiles', plot real time along horizontal axis instead of short minutes (fast time). Goods Train 1 leaves Station C at 0 minutes and stops at Station B at 25 minutes to shunt and to allow Train 2, a non-stopping passenger train, to pass. Train 1 also waits on Siding D to allow Train 3 to pass. Train 2 reaches Station C and is turned to become Train 4 leaving 5 minutes later. Train 3 is a goods train which stops at Station B to shunt and to allow Train 4 to pass.

Average speed of a train is given by the slope.

Train 2 travels 12 smiles from A to C in 30 fast minutes — average speed thus 24 miles per hour.

Schematic track diagram

Short minutes

The train graph

Above *Once we have established our standard timetable we can increase the operating activity by adding extra unscheduled trains. An interesting example is an enthusiast's special which will give us the opportunity to run a locomotive and stock which might otherwise be inappropriate to the line. This scene was specially set up on the Isle of Purbeck MRC's 00-gauge Swanage branch layout with a Triang 'Lord of the Isles' heading the train.* **Below** *Another instance where a special unscheduled train can add to the interest of timetable operation. This is the snowplough train, rather rarely required in Britain, but regularly needed on many European and American lines in the winter. This train is on a Swiss narrow-gauge line.*

operators to use, and these can be marked to show the features of importance to the particular operator. For example, if one operator is concerned with running an intermediate junction station on the line, a red line can be drawn horizontally across the graph at the level of the station. It is then easy for that operator to see exactly when the various trains reach his station as this will be where the train lines cut the red line. Alternatively, if one operator will be running certain trains then on his copy of the train graph his trains can have their lines marked in red. The train graphs represent a point to point system but can also be applied to an oval layout perfectly satisfactorily. In this case one point on the oval (perhaps one station or yard, or, best of all, if there are hidden sidings at one side of the oval serving as a fiddle yard) is included at both the top and the bottom of the vertical axis of the graph. To avoid confusion it can be named differently for the two positions. Once a train has arrived at this point it can either reverse forming a train returning from this yard or it can go on when it will be a new train starting at the other end of the axis on the train graph.

Ideally, the train graph is constructed, as mentioned above, with distance plotted on the vertical axis, positioning stations and other points accurately on this axis according to their situation on the layout, measuring in scale miles, actual feet or 'smiles'. We can then plot the train lines exactly either working from the times we want the trains to be at particular points, or on the basis of the speed, because the slope of the train lines relates to the speed — the faster the train the more nearly vertical the train line. Thus working from the time the train leaves a station we can determine by drawing in the appropriate slope when it will reach the next station travelling at the speed we have chosen. This may, for example, be 60 scale miles per hour for a passenger train, and only 20 miles per hour for a slow goods train.

However, if we want to keep things simple and do not wish to measure the distances on the layout, or calculate them in terms of scale miles, it is still possible to construct a train graph by working more empirically. To do this we run the various trains we intend to include in the timetable over the layout. Taking care to run them at what appear to the eye to be suitable scale speeds, each journey is carefully timed for each point on the trip and these are noted down. We then construct a train graph as before but, instead of plotting distances on the vertical axis, we merely list the stations on the route in their correct order along this axis. They can either be spaced evenly regardless of their actual distances apart or they can be placed approximately as they are located in relation to each other on the layout. Such a graph will not yield all the information that the more accurately plotted one will; we cannot, for example, calculate the train speed from the slope of the train line. However, the graph can still be a very useful method of constructing a suitable timetable for operating the layout and a helpful visual presentation of that timetable for the operators.

So far both in simple timetable construction and in the train graph we have been concerned only with the scheduled trains which are run regularly on the layout. After a time when the timetable becomes very familiar and perhaps a little repetitious, some enthusiasts like to add a little extra challenge and interest to the proceedings by introducing unscheduled extra trains and other complications. The need to cope with these, while at the same time interfering as little as possible with the regular trains on the timetable will certainly stop the operators getting bored! One method of introducing these complications at random, thus making the session more exciting, is to have a set of cards, sometimes called situation or hazard cards, on each of which is listed a situation which will affect operation. These can include changes in the traffic needs necessitating the running of an extra train or of providing additional coaches for one which is already scheduled, breakdowns or derailments which may entail delays or diversions as well as the making up of a breakdown train and running it to the location, and so on. The list of possibilities is almost limitless and you can easily select some which are appropriate to your layout. The cards are shuffled and the pack is placed face down. Then, at predetermined times during an operating session, a card can be taken from the top of the pack and the instructions carried out. The introduction of unscheduled events at random in this way can do a great deal to add interest and challenge to a session, even if the basic timetable is becoming rather routine.

The train graph

Bell codes

On the prototype railway bell signals sent from one signal box to the next advise the signalmen of the trains passing into the areas which they control. The messages are passed in a code system with which the signalmen are as familiar as a radio operator is with the morse code. Rather than merely exchanging information by direct conversation, some railway modellers like to use the standard British Rail bell signalling codes for communication between two or more operators running a model railway layout. The system is not only convenient, particularly if the layout is a large one with the operators some distance apart, perhaps even in different rooms, but is also authentic, adding realism to operating procedures.

The prototype codes are designed to cover every possible contingency, and are further complicated by the fact that some codes apply to all British Rail regions, some to all regions

Below *Part of the fiddle yard on Eric Kay's N-gauge Sherrington branch. The fiddle yard operator uses the gong at the right to communicate by bell code with the other operator at the station. Note the check list showing the codes commonly used on the layout.* **Below right** *Simple bell code system as used on the Sherrington Branch.*

except the Southern, and some to the Southern Region only! For the full details I would refer you to the very useful book, *British Railway Signalling* by G.M. Kichenside and Alan Williams, published by Ian Allan, where the BR Standard Signal Box Bell Codes are given in full in an appendix. Most modellers find that a restricted code is adequate for their needs and is much easier to learn, so that operators quickly find they no longer have to keep referring back to the list. As an example, the bell code presented here is the one that Eric Kay used on his Sherrington Branch and which proved perfectly adequate for normal operation, both at home and at exhibitions. When there were two operators on his layout, one would man the terminus station, Sherrington, and the other the fiddle yard and the bell code was employed for communication between them to offer and accept trains.

I would advise the beginner who would like to use the bell code system to start with a simple selection, rather than with too full a list which will be difficult to use. It is easy to add further codes as necessary later. The actual bells can be merely bell gongs, struck by hand, or an electric bell system can be installed, arranged so that each press of a button or switch gives a single ring.

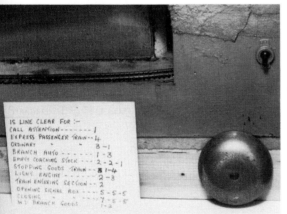

Opening signal box	5-5-5
Closing signal box	7-5-5
Call Attention	1
Is line clear for:	
Express passenger train	4
Ordinary passenger train	3-1
Branch auto-train	1-3
Empty coaching stock	2-2-1
Light Engine	2-3
Train entering section	2
Branch goods train	1-2

Card order systems

In looking at operation on a model railway layout, so far we have concentrated on the movement of complete trains, passenger and freight, over the line in accordance with a schedule. We have considered how to compile a timetable based on a realistic pattern of operation to handle the traffic appropriate to the line. As yet we have not taken into account the distribution of individual goods wagons, vans and other stock. On a branch line we have merely sent a goods train made up from what appears to be a reasonable selection of stock from the fiddle yard to the terminus. At this destination we have perhaps exchanged the incoming wagons for ones already at the station and which are assumed to be ready to go back to the junction (fiddle yard).

While recognising that it is desirable for realism that our goods stock should appear to be moving in response to the traffic needs, we have no automatic method of producing an authentic traffic flow and must either improvise as we go or have a set scheme laid down for our sequence operation or timetable. Neither system is ideal. The former tends to lead to any wagons which are not easy to get at, being ignored when shunting is carried out, while the latter is likely to become too well known to the operator in time, making operation too predictable and, therefore, less interesting. On the prototype railways the needs of the customers dictate the traffic and, as these needs fluctuate, so the goods traffic varies, but we have no customers on our model railway.

In an effort to create, artificially, realistic and varying goods traffic in model railway operation, a number of systems of freight car distribution have been devised. I use the American term 'freight car' deliberately because there has been a particular interest in this subject in the United States and most of the schemes have originated there. The systems have been designed to represent American prototype railroad practice, particularly the operations of the 'way freight' train which travels the single track main line stopping to drop and pick up cars at numerous stations and lineside industries. However, the schemes can also be applied with good effect on British layouts with only minor adaptations. Freight car distribution systems are ideal for small shunting layouts such as those based on industrial railways and can create very interesting operation on a small layout. On other lines, for example a country branch, the systems can be used in combination with a timetable, and will provide the basis for the distribution of goods stock to and from the terminus and any intermediate stations or lineside industries by the trains listed in the schedule.

In one of the simplest forms of random distribution selection, modellers have used playing cards, deciding beforehand which card or cards from the pack will represent which destination for the rolling stock. When the train is ready to depart the cards are shuffled and dealt from the top of the pack. The first card shows where the first wagon is to go, the second card the second wagon, and so on. As all destinations will not be appropriate for all wagons it will be necessary on occasions to ignore the card turned up for a particular wagon and to turn up others until a suitable one is found.

A variant which will overcome the problem of unsuitable destinations is to have groups of destinations, each of which can accept any wagon. For example, one group could be made up of several industrial sidings. If a wagon is directed here it can be shunted onto a siding which is appropriate for use. Another group may be a goods yard with various facilities; thus a cattle wagon directed to the goods yard would be put on the siding serving the cattle dock. If we have four groups we can, as suggested by Mr Evens in *Model Railways* magazine (January 1974) use a pack of cards with the court cards removed and use the categories of cards red-even, red-odd, black-even, and black-odd, to give the four groups.

The true card order systems, however, do not rely on playing cards but have cards, one for each wagon on the railway, on which enough information to identify each individual wagon,

```
OWNER:    HIGHLEY MINING COMPANY.
TYPE:     10 TON OPEN WAGON.
NO.       425.

DESTINATION:

Colliery.

Coal Staithes.

Smiths Factory.

Crowley Manufacturing Company.

Johnson's Foundry.

Fiddle Yard.
```

A wagon card for a simple card order system. A paper clip is used as a marker to indicate destination on left.

van, tanker, etc, is provided. There are many ways in which distribution of the rolling stock can then be organised. One simple system is to have another set of cards with all possible destinations, again one card for each. The two sets of cards are shuffled separately and the top card from each is turned up providing a wagon and its destination. This process is then repeated as many times as there are to be wagons in the train. Again there may be the problem of inappropriate destinations turning up with the need to go on to another card. A similar system could be employed to determine which wagons the train picks up, or alternatively, one wagon could be collected for each one dropped.

Another scheme is to include on each wagon card a note of the appropriate load and the origin and destination for that load. The cards belonging to the wagons which are at a particular station are kept in a small box at the station. When a train arrives the driver takes a number of cards from the box, collects the wagons concerned, and takes them, and their cards, to the appropriate destinations; if a wagon begins at its destination then it is returned to its origin as an empty. The number of cards taken can be at the driver's discretion, or previously decided, or determined at the time by throwing a dice. This system in its simplest form will mean that any particular wagon will only move between two places, origin to destination and back. A more interesting variant is to have all the possible destinations for a particular wagon listed across the top or along one side of the card and to select one of these, indicating which with a paper clip, before the run.

There are many variants of the card order system but I would like to describe one simple system which can be applied to a small layout and which you may find suitable for your

model railway. If you do employ it you should find it a useful basis, though as you gain experience you will probably wish to make modifications to suit the particular features of your line.

Strictly, card order systems should apply to loads and allow for whether or not a wagon, van, etc is empty or loaded, but if we concern ourselves only with rolling stock movements we can simplify the system to advantage. The method can be applied to a fiddle yard to terminus layout, to a through station type of layout with a fiddle yard at each end, or to an oval continuous scheme. Obviously the more stations, sidings and industries that we can include on the layout, the greater will be the scope for stock distribution and the more entertaining the operation.

The initial step is to list all the possible destinations including goods sidings of various types at different stations and any industries at these stations or along the line. A card (a plain postcard is suitable) is made out for each item of goods rolling stock on the railway indicating its type, number and, in the case of Private Owner stock, the name of the owner, to help easy identification during operation. Below this list the possible destinations. If you have a layout with one or more through stations and a yard or fiddle yard at each end, or a continuous layout with part concealed and used as a fiddle yard for trains coming either way round the oval, you can also include TGA and TGB at regular intervals in the listings, standing for 'Through Goods' with the 'A' or 'B' indicating the direction of travel along or around the track. In this case the wagon will be taken through to the yard at the other end of the journey and will wait there until another train is made up. At each station, yard or industrial site there will be a box for cards, divided into an arrivals side and a departures side. If there are several sidings at that point the two sides will each be subdivided into sections for each siding. These boxes can easily be made from stout card with thinner card for the subdividing pieces.

When we start an operating session the stock will normally be spread around the layout on various sidings and the card for each wagon will be in the box at the site at which the wagon is located. We can make up a train in the yard or fiddle yard by taking the required number of cards from the box there and then assembling the wagons concerned in the yard. On each card there will be a paper clip marking one of the destinations and the operator distributes the stock from the train into the indicated sidings as the train makes its journey along the line. On arrival at a siding for which his train has a wagon the driver looks in the box. If there is a card, or cards, in the departures section he removes this and then transfers any card in the arrivals section into the departures side. The card or cards for any wagons to be dropped at the siding he places in the arrivals side. After carrying out the necessary shunting to drop and pick up wagons as required, the driver takes his train on, together with the remaining cards from his original selection, plus the cards for any wagons he has picked up here. On the cards he picks up he moves the paper clips down to the next destination on the list. If it is on his route he can drop these wagons, if not he takes them through to the yard at the end of the journey where they will wait for a train in the other direction.

In fact there are quite a number of variations possible regarding picking up wagons. One frequently used is to only pick up wagons that are to travel in the direction of the train; others are left for the first train in the opposite direction. Some modellers like to pick up the same number of wagons at a siding as are dropped there; this has the advantage of balancing the stock around the layout automatically. Although on this system each wagon runs through the same pattern of distribution repeatedly, the clip being moved back to the top of the list when it reaches the bottom, the number of destinations on the

cards will vary from wagon to wagon so there will be almost limitless variation in the way trains are made up, especially if there are a reasonable number of wagons and destinations. Variety can also be added by listing destinations in differing orders on the various cards.

Though this system is a fairly simple one I think you will find that it gives a sense of purpose to the running of goods trains on your layout. No longer are you just picking up a few wagons here and there as the mood takes you, and for no particular reason; instead you are moving wagons following the instructions given providing a fair representation of the real railway, responding to the needs of its customers.

One of the main criticisms of the card order systems is the need for the cards to be carried by the driver from place to place with the train, and the difficulty of marrying up a wagon with its card again if the two become separated. In fact these problems only really apply on large layouts with numerous wagons and with considerable actual distances between different parts of the layout. On a small layout a simple card order system, as described above, should be perfectly satisfactory. On some layouts, in an attempt to overcome the problems just mentioned, systems have been devised where the freight car itself carries either a slip of paper or a drawing pin, the head of which is coloured according to a code, which tells the operator where it is to go.

Cliff Young, a modeller living in Britain but modelling American prototype, uses a card and waybill system for freight operation based on one devised by an American modeller, Doug Smith, but modified to suit his own requirements. The system is more complicated than the simple one I described above but correspondingly is more flexible and realistic. He has given details of his system in an article in the November 1966 issue of *Railway Modeller* magazine and also in the recently published book *The Encyclopaedia of Model Railways* from Octopus Books Ltd, and I would recommend that readers interested in taking the subject further should consult his articles.

Card order systems

Loading and unloading

As we have already seen, for realism in the operation of a model railway layout we must give the impression that it is actually transporting people and goods from place to place, reproducing in miniature the function of the prototype. However, because our miniature railway workers cannot load and unload our wagons and vans for us, we do run into problems with appearances in this respect. So often on model railways we see a train arrive and shunt a wagon loaded with coal on to a siding, only to have the wagon taken away again by the next train still full of coal! With much of our rolling stock there is, of course, no difficulty. Though a few modellers do include passengers inside model coaches, it is not generally very noticeable whether coaches are full or empty so we can consider them as whichever we need according to the requirements of our timetable. And there is obviously nothing we can do to simulate passengers getting on and off the trains! Similarly with goods stock such as vans, tankers, cement wagons, salt wagons, and so on, the loaded and empty stock appears identical. If we wish to preserve the correct procedures we can shunt vans into a goods shed or under a canopy outside the door of a warehouse, tankers can be positioned alongside storage tanks, cement wagons beneath a hopper, and so on, where we can imagine loading or unloading is taking place without distorting realism too much.

The difficulty comes with open wagons,

timber bolsters, flat wagons, and suchlike. Some modellers just load and unload openly by hand, ignoring appearances for the short time taken. If you are exhibiting your layout you may prefer to arrange things so this procedure takes place out of sight of the public. One possibility is to run the stock into a goods shed, warehouse or factory building which has no back so that you have access to the interior for loading and unloading without viewers being aware of this. Alternatively you may be able to run the stock on to a hidden siding or to the fiddle yard. Whatever you do, the process of loading and unloading is made much easier with specially made loads. For an open wagon, cut a rectangle of balsa or thick card to fit neatly into the top of the wagon. On top of this glue the coal, rock chippings, sand, barrels, sacks, boxes, or whatever other load you wish to represent. On the underside glue a small block of wood, of the right size to support the load at the correct level inside the wagon, at the centre. This arrangement makes it easy to remove the load; merely pressing on one end will cause it to tilt so that you can pick it up. Replacing the load is also easy and, of course, the loads can be used for different wagons provided the dimensions are the same.

A system which can be very realistic if we are modelling trains transporting bulk loads between two places, for example, ore being taken from a mine to a processing plant, is to have two trains which are identical, except for the fact that one has full wagons and the other empty wagons. With the arrangement of the tracks it appears that loaded trains are emerging from the mine and running into the processing plant, while the reverse is taking place with the empty trains.

There are also a number of working model loaders of various types now available as kits or ready-to-use models and, with these, wagons can actually be loaded and unloaded adding to the realism of operation. An example is the Faller Gravel Works complete with storage silos, working conveyor belts and operating hopper wagons.

Removable wagon load with narrow central support beneath false floor. Pressing at one end tilts load for easy removal.

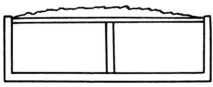

Above *The marshalling sidings of the hump shunting yard at the Tyne Yard. Though, obviously, considerable simplification and compression is necessary, an interesting and realistic hump yard can be included on a large or moderate sized model railway layout.* **Below** *A van passing through a retarder on the Tyne Yard hump yard.*

Loading and unloading

Two views of an operating model hump yard on a large HO-scale Fleischmann exhibition layout. **Top** *The hump itself is in the centre of this picture.* **Above** *The five marshalling sidings of the hump yard are shown in the right centre of this photograph. On this automatically operated layout, wagons are distributed at random on to these sidings.* **Below** *Part of the track plan of the HO-scale Fleischmann exhibition layout. The small black triangle near the left side indicates the site of the hump, the lap point (three-way) is labelled 227, and the five tracks of the marshalling yard are in the central part of the diagram.* (Courtesy of Fleischmann.)

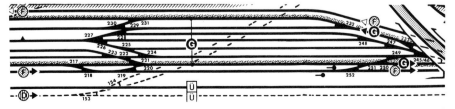

One of the most interesting aspects of the handling of freight traffic on modern prototype railways is the marshalling of wagons and vans in hump yards. Models of these yards are not often seen though the Reverend Edward Beal built one for his well-known West Midland layout nearly 30 years ago! Real hump yards occupy a great deal of space but considerable compression is possible for a model and, while one could not be included on a small layout, it would be possible to fit one in on a moderate sized home or club layout if desired. The accompanying photographs show an HO-scale working hump yard, automatically operated, on a large Fleischmann exhibition layout. An interesting point is that the yard was built entirely with standard Fleischmann parts. The single track passing over the hump has an uncoupler on the slope beyond the hump after which it divides into three by a lap point. The outer two tracks then divide again by ordinary turnouts giving a total of five marshalling sidings on which the trains are assembled. By means of contacts on the tracks, wagons passing along the tracks change the points for the following wagons.

Shunting competitions

With many systems the operating of a model railway layout can be considered as a form of game, with the challenge of keeping the layout running efficiently while overcoming any complications which arise or are deliberately introduced, all the time obeying the rules and trying to maintain realism. Part of the skill developed in operating relates to shunting, so that with practice the enthusiast becomes better both at planning his moves and at actually carrying them out smoothly, realistically and efficiently. Taking this a little further some modellers have produced small shunting modules designed to be used as a form of competitive game. One of the most successful of these was devised by John Allen, who was a very well-known American modeller. Basically the track plan is a run-around loop with a selection of sidings and the aim is to distribute a number of freight cars placed on the module in accordance with a pre-set plan. There are many different ways in which the module can be used and the game has proved very popular.

Often with puzzles of this sort the number of moves taken are counted but John Allen chose instead to arrange for a constant slow locomotive speed and for the competition to be carried out against the clock. Thus it is important to be quick rather than to take the least possible number of moves. Used in its original form the module was very interesting but a further development was to build a mirror image unit and to link the two, so that two people can operate, one on each module, at the same time. Though the two could compete against each other, the game is carried out with them trying to help each other so that their time is taken as the time for both to have completed the required moves.

Shunting games of this type have great potential for entertainment and also for practice in operation. Full details of John Allen's layout were given in the November 1972 issue of *Model Railroader* magazine and anyone contemplating building such a module might like to refer to that article.

Loading and unloading

Maintenance

If the model railway layout is to provide interesting, enjoyable and realistic operation it is essential that the models should work well. Even for very simple operation poor running, frequent derailments, coupling faults and other interruptions will spoil the fun and may well cause the modeller to lose interest. Most of the ready-to-run equipment now available is of very good quality, but, for continued good running, regular maintenance is necessary. Some modellers neglect such attention because they feel it will be an uninteresting and time-consuming chore, others, particularly beginners, because they do not know how to tackle the job. Undeniably on a large and complex layout a great deal of time must be spent on cleaning, checking, adjusting and repairing and this is one of the reasons why the beginner should be careful not to attempt to build too ambitious a model railway layout. If

he does manage to complete such a model he may find that he has so much maintenance to do he has little time left to sit back and operate his railway. However, on a smaller, simpler layout even the beginner should be able to carry out these important tasks quickly and easily and there is no doubt that the enjoyment and satisfaction obtained from the consequent smooth, reliable running will more than compensate for the time and effort.

Obviously prevention is always better than cure, in railway modelling as well as in medicine! Much can be done to avoid future troubles by good initial construction and by care in handling, operating and storing locomotives, rolling stock, track, structures and other items. Care of your models is very important and right from the beginning, with the train set, it is worth getting into good habits. After all the standard of many ready-to-

Below *Maintenance vehicles are important on the full size railways. This SR two-car electric set is a rail cleaning and de-icing unit.* **Below right** *A re-railer makes the placing of rolling stock on the rails easier and is especially useful for N-gauge bogie rolling stock. Because it makes it easier to re-rail stock less handling is likely to be necessary and there is therefore less risk of accidental damage. In this picture an Eggerbahn re-railer is being used to place a Peco N-gauge tank wagon on the track.*

run models is now so good that you may well want to retain them for use on a scale layout. Alternatively, if you come to sell or exchange them you will get a better deal if they are in good condition and have clearly been properly looked after. With the train set, track and points can easily be broken, twisted or bent when setting up or dismantling the layout if due care is not taken. Do not hold pieces of track in mid air when fitting them together as this may lead to twisting and distortion of the pieces with consequent derailments. Instead, place the two track sections on a flat surface and slide them together. Never force together any pieces you are having difficulty with. Instead look carefully to see why they will not join up. Damage may also occur during storage between operating sessions, particularly if the models and track are just dumped into a large box, drawer or cupboard. The models can be conveniently and safely stored in their original boxes when not in use. Many manufacturers now include a pre-formed plastic packing piece into which the locomotive or item of rolling stock fits snugly within the box, and this helps to avoid damage. Alternatively, if the boxes are no longer available you can wrap the models in paper, preferably tissue paper, but newspaper will do, and pack them carefully into a box. Take special care not to damage couplings or wheels. Small detail fittings are also especially vulnerable. Pack track sections face to face in pairs in a box with the points on top. Slight, almost unnoticeable damage to or twisting of the track pieces may lead to troubles in running for which there is no apparent cause, so take the time and trouble to protect them during storage by proper packing. While considering the train set it is worth mentioning that, though you may have to lay the set out on

the floor you should not put it down on carpet if you can avoid doing so because fluff and dirt from the carpet will quickly get on to the wheels and axles and into the mechanisms.

One of the major problems for the railway modeller is the dust so often present in the atmosphere. Airborne dust and dirt are a nuisance in many ways affecting both the appearance and the performance of a model railway layout. In most rooms a deposit of dust settles over a layout in a surprisingly short time, even if the layout is in fairly regular use. It is especially noticeable on locomotives and rolling stock but soon makes the scenery and structures appear grimy also. The real thing is, of course, exposed to dirt, grime, dust and rain giving a weathered look which we try hard to duplicate to make our models realistic, but unfortunately the dust which settles on the layout does not give this effect but instead merely looks dirty!

Dust also interferes with the smooth running of our models in various ways. Dirt from the air becomes trapped in the oil or grease used to lubricate gearboxes and bearings and causes wear while dust deposits on electrical contacts and on the rails interfere with current flow making operation erratic. We can tackle the problem in two basic ways; preventing dust from reaching the railway and removing any which does. Ideally, the layout should be in an atmosphere as free of dust as possible. However, most railway modellers are only too pleased to find anywhere to put a model railway and cannot afford to be too choosy about the room where they set up their layout. Often a bedroom is the only possibility and, unfortunately, is particularly bad from this point of view as the bedclothes give rise to a lot of dust and fluff, most of which seems to find

Maintenance

its way on to the layout! Even in the lounge there is a good deal of dust from the furnishings as people move about the room, sit in the chairs, draw the curtains, and so on. The ideal is a room set aside solely for the layout, but few of us are this fortunate. If you are lucky enough to have a model railway room, plastic or lino floor tiles or covering, rather than a carpet, will reduce the amount of dust. If you want to cover in the space beneath the layout, hardboard panels are a better choice than old curtain material which is likely to harbour dust and dirt. The room should be kept as clean as possible and any sanding, filing, sawing or other work which produces dust should, if possible, be done elsewhere. Some American modellers, more accustomed to air conditioning than we are in Britain, have experimented with fans and filter-blower units in an attempt to keep dust out of the layout room but such arrangements are more elaborate and expensive than most modellers would wish to consider using.

If we cannot exclude dust from the room we can try to keep it off the layout itself. The difficulty is that most model railways are rather large compared to other types of models. It is much easier for car, ship and military modellers, for example, to put their creations into small cases or into bookcases or cabinets to keep them away from dust and dirt. Cabinets or cases of this type, preferably with glass doors, can be ideal for storing locomotives and rolling stock safely away from dust and from the risk of damage. They are easily and quickly accessible when wanted for operating and, if the doors are fitted with glass, the models can be seen by the modeller and by visitors without the need for handling. A few modellers have built small enclosed layouts, usually in the form of coffee tables with glass tops, occasionally in glass cases. An example of a small layout built into a coffee table is the 009 narrow gauge model railway constructed by Mr K.J. Churms which was illustrated in *PSL Model Railway Guides 1* and *2*. Such an arrangement creates an interesting and attractive piece of furniture and also keeps most of the dust out. However, unless the layout is very carefully sealed up, a little dust will creep in and the model will require occasional cleaning.

Covering larger layouts is less convenient but is certainly desirable unless the room is relatively dust free. The easiest and cheapest method is probably to use a sheet of clear polythene. Some form of support to hold the sheet clear of the structures, scenery and details is desirable as otherwise they are likely to be damaged by the cover as it is fitted or removed. A convenient method is to use hoops

bent up from wire and fitted on beneath the polythene. The cover will not be airtight so some dust will get under it, but it will help by keeping out most of the dust. The plastic will become dirty and should be washed from time to time. Covering and uncovering the layout for operating takes only a few minutes and is more than compensated for by the time saved in cleaning.

An even better scheme is some form of hinged lid which covers the layout when not in use but is easily raised for operation. Such an arrangement does require more work to construct and the materials needed will be more expensive. The details will depend on your layout size and shape. The Reverend Peter Denny constructed a very neat hinged cover for his Buckingham Branch layout some years ago using wood, hardboard and strawboard. His cover was counterweighted and was also fitted with lights, giving good illumination of the layout when in operation. A detailed description of the cover and its construction was given in the June 1961 issue of *Railway Modeller* magazine and I would recommend that you refer to this if you are considering making a cover of this type for your layout.

If the only place available for a model railway layout is in a room which is regularly used for other purposes such as the lounge, hall or a bedroom, an excellent arrangement is to build the layout into a piece of furniture such as a bookcase or a chest of drawers. The top can be hinged so that, when not in operation, the railway can be concealed by closing the lid, making the unit look like an ordinary piece of furniture. This system also protects the layout from accidental damage and, to a considerable extent, from dust and dirt. Ron Prattley has built a fine example of a bookcase containing an 00-gauge layout for his lounge. He made the lid removable so that it could be reversed to form an extension to the fixed part of the layout in the bookcase. The fiddle yard is a further detachable piece which fits as a drawer in the bookcase when the railway is not in use, and is illustrated in the *PSL Model Railway Guide 1: Baseboards, Track and Electrification.*

Another method sometimes employed by modellers who are short of space for a layout is to hinge the baseboard on to a wall or into a unit of furniture so that the railway can be folded down for operating and then swung up against the wall, or into the cabinet or cupboard out of the way when the running session is over. This scheme also has advantages from the point of view of keeping the layout clean as less dust will settle on it while it is standing on edge, particularly if it swings up into a unit of furniture so that there

Above *Harold Bowcott's 00-gauge layout is hinged on to the wall so that when not in use it can be stored folded up out of the way. This arrangement also helps to keep the layout clean as much less dust will settle on it in the vertical position. Shelves on the wall, arranged to fit into the operating well when the layout is folded up, provide storage for locomotives and rolling stock. (Photograph by Brian Monaghan.)* **Below** *A British Rail ballast cleaner. All the railway modeller needs is a vacuum cleaner and a soft brush!*

is a covering strip above it. Harold Bowcott has constructed an 00-gauge layout which is hinged on to the wall so that it can be folded up against it, thus taking up a minimum of space when not in use. This position also keeps most of the dust off the layout.

In addition to keeping as much dust and dirt as possible away from the layout it is also important to avoid extremes of temperature, direct sunlight and damp as these can cause damage, warping, fading of the colours, and even melting of plastic structures and other items. For these reasons, sites such as lofts, where temperatures may vary greatly, cellars, garages and garden sheds, all of which may be damp, should be considered carefully before

building a layout there to make sure that conditions will be acceptable. All these locations are also inclined to be dirty and dusty unless properly finished inside.

For general cleaning of the layout a vacuum cleaner with a nozzle attachment fitted is ideal. There is no need to touch the layout with the nozzle, it can be held an inch or two above the surface thus avoiding the risk of damage. If you wish you can cover the nozzle end with wire mesh so that if any small details, such as figures, have become detached from the layout surface they will be caught by the mesh and not sucked up into the cleaner bag. A soft brush may be needed for more persistent dust, especially on structures. For locomotives and

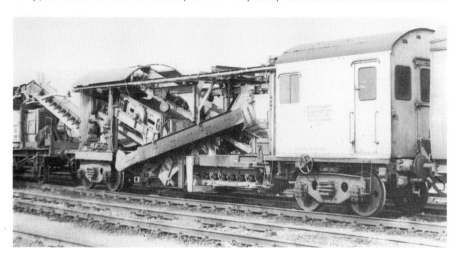

Above *Eric Kay made this track cleaning wagon from an Atlas N-scale railroad car by drilling a hole in the floor to take the plastic nozzle and fixing a foam rubber pad beneath the floor. Track cleaning fluid poured into the nozzle soaks the pad and cleans the track as the car moves along the track. Lead weights fixed inside the car apply pressure on the pad.* **Below left** *This neat electric outline locomotive model is the Fleischmann N-scale track cleaning locomotive.* **Below right** *This view of the underside of the Fleischmann N-scale track cleaning locomotive clearly shows the two pads which clean the rails as the model runs on the track.*

rolling stock a small soft brush is useful for cleaning ; a convenient brush to use is one of the type sometimes employed for cleaning camera lenses and interiors in which the brush is combined with a rubber puffer so that dust in crevices can be blown out. This enables easy cleaning without risk of damage to small details. Even with fairly regular cleaning of the scenery the colours tend to become dull and dingy after a while and repainting may be necessary eventually. Lichen used for modelling bushes and trees may become brittle in time and it is then likely to crumble if touched. Its pliability can be restored by spraying it with a mixture of one part glycerine to three parts of water.

Track cleaning is especially important as it affects operation as well as appearance. Regular running of the trains does much to help keep the rails clean on their running surfaces, but most of us cannot run our trains often enough for this alone to be sufficient. In addition we will need to clean the rails with a little solvent fairly regularly to remove oil and dirt. The solvent can be methylated spirits or one of the commercially available track cleaners on the market. It can be applied with a soft piece of cloth or with a track cleaning wagon. Several manufacturers produce model wagons or vans which actually clean the track, either by means of a foam pad or by one or two rotating pads beneath the vehicle. In addition Fleischmann make a track cleaning locomotive in N gauge. Some modellers use WD 40 for

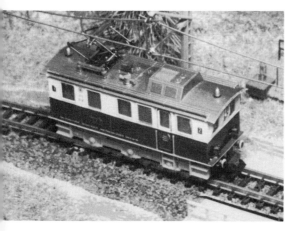

track cleaning and this is effective but, as it is a little oily, it should be kept off the track surroundings. For more vigorous cleaning, perhaps when the layout has not been run for some time, a track cleaning rubber such as that made by Peco can be employed. Do not use abrasives such as sandpaper or emery cloth as these will leave scratches on the rails which predispose to the accumulation of more dirt with a recurrence of the problems. Points should also be carefully cleaned including the backs of the blades and stock rails to ensure good electrical contact. Make sure that there is no dirt or loose ballast preventing full movement of the point blades. Remove any fluff which is caught up on the rails and brush away any dust. Also check the frog for any build up of dirt deposits. When cleaning the track check also for any loose track pins, any loss of alignment at track joins and for loose fishplates, and carry out any repairs needed.

A recently introduced device which maintains good electrical conduction, even if the track is dirty, is the Relco High Frequency Generator. This unit uses high frequency superimposed on the normal supply to ionise the gap due to dirt on the track and restore electrical contact. The device converts the 12-volt DC input into high frequency AC only when the circuit is broken, burning away the dirt and restoring conductivity. The normal DC current then flows again. The generator is easily wired into the layout input and is perfectly safe to use.

It is also worth mentioning that the Multiple Train Control systems now on the market from Airfix and Hornby are less affected by dirty track than the conventional system because of the higher voltage employed and because it is constantly applied. On the ordinary 12-volt DC system the actual voltage applied is often much lower than 12 volts. I understand that the Relco HF Generator must not be used with the Multiple Train Control systems.

The full benefits of track cleaning will not be realised unless you also clean the wheels of your locomotives and rolling stock. Dirt collects on locomotive wheels and interferes with electrical pick-up; it can also spread from

Top right *When the layout has not been operated recently the use of a track cleaning rubber such as that made by Peco is an effective way of cleaning the rails.* **Above right** *A pipe cleaner with the tip dipped into methylated spirits or other track cleaner is useful for cleaning points.* **Right** *A Relco HF Generator for track cleaning.*

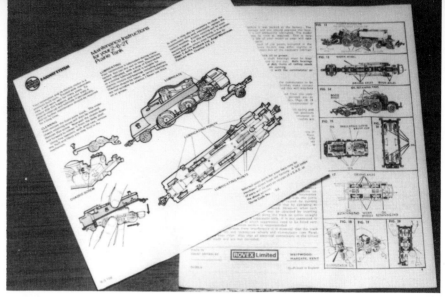

Above *The manufacturers issue instruction sheets for their locomotives and other models detailing how lubrication and maintenance should be carried out and the modeller should study the relevant information carefully. The examples shown here are from Airfix and Hornby.* **Right** *A van derailed at Gävle on the Swedish State Railway system. When any incident of this type occurs on the prototype railways a careful check is made to determine the cause. On a model railway layout we need not be so painstaking but if repeated derailments occur at the same spot or with the same piece of rolling stock then some investigation is called for.*

the wheels on to the track. For cleaning locomotive driving wheels Peco make a wheel cleaning brush and scraper set which is very effective. The wires from the brush and scraper are connected either to the 12-volt power unit terminals or to the track and, when the brush and scraper are applied to the driving wheels, one on each side, the wheels rotate making cleaning easy and effective. Sometimes scraping with a small screwdriver is necessary to remove firmly adherent dirt. On rolling stock wheels the dirt has less direct effect on running but it will spread on to the track so cleaning the rolling stock wheels is also important. Gentle scraping with a small screwdriver is the most effective method. Also look for fluff and hairs wound round axles and in bearings on both locomotives and rolling stock and remove them with a needle point and a pair of fine tweezers.

Generally locomotive mechanisms require relatively little attention and, if running well, they should, for the most part, be left well alone. Most are ready to run when purchased and do not even need oiling. In fact, many more problems arise from over oiling model locomotives than from them having insufficient lubrication. It is particularly important to avoid getting oil onto the commutator or brushes of the motor. The correct type of oil should be used; do not use thick oil or grease. Some oils can damage plastic so it is advisable to use one of the oils especially marketed for railway

modelling such as Peco Electrolube. The instruction leaflets provided by the manufacturer will indicate the lubricating points on the locomotive concerned and you should follow the advice given in these instructions. Only apply a tiny drop of oil at each point. These include the axle bearings, the coupling rod pins, valve gear pivots, and the felt oil retaining pads on the armature shaft bearing.

From time to time it may be necessary to clean the slots between the segments of the commutator as carbon from the brushes accumulates here and interferes with smooth running. To do this the brush pressure on the commutator is relieved or the brushes are removed and a wooden toothpick can then be used to remove the deposit. It is important not to scratch the surface of the commutator or the armature windings. Any oil on the commutator should be wiped off with a clean rag. If the brushes are worn they can be replaced at this time.

If you are in any doubt about your ability to carry out any of these jobs do take the model to your local dealer rather than risk causing damage. Always read the instruction leaflets carefully before doing anything to your model locomotives. Never take them apart just for the sake of it if they are running satisfactorily and never remove the magnet from the motor as it will lose its power unless it is kept in contact with a keeper all the time.

If a locomotive will not run, though it has operated satisfactorily previously, this may be due to there being no power to the track or to a fault in the locomotive or its electrical pick-up. A simple means of checking for a fault in the supply to the track is to try another locomotive on the same piece of track. If this will not run either make sure that the power is actually switched on and that there are no loose connections between the power unit and the track. Also check that the fishplates are tight and providing proper electrical contact. Never fiddle with the mains side of the power unit and never open the power unit casing, as accidents with the mains supply can be fatal. If you suspect a fault here take the unit to your local dealer for expert advice.

If the track is not at fault we need to check the locomotive. Remove the body and apply wires from the 12-volt DC output of the power unit direct to the brushes, one to each. The motor will then usually run. If so, then the current is not reaching the motor from the track and this may be due to dirty wheels, a pick-up not in contact with its wheel, or a lead which has come loose. It is usually fairly easy to spot which of these is the cause. If, when the wires are applied to the brushes, the motor moves only slightly, it suggests that the problem is mechanical, either due to binding or breakage, or due to hairs and fluff wound round the axles and bearings. If there is no sign of life in the motor when the wires are applied

and the brushes are in good condition, then it would appear to be the motor which is at fault and you will need to take the model to your local dealer for attention.

The best way of maintaining your model railway in good working order, with a minimum of effort, is to carry out the necessary servicing and repairs regularly. If you set aside part of an operating session each week or two for these jobs you will find that only a short time will usually be required, whereas if you let too many jobs accumulate, you will be in for a long session when you eventually get round to attending to them. In the meantime your railway will not be running as well as it should.

Some modellers like to keep a notebook to list any faults which they notice during operating sessions so that they do not forget them when they have a maintenance and repair session. One system which has advantages, especially on a large layout with several operators, is to have some way of marking points on the track at which derailments occur and the locomotives or stock concerned. If several markers accumulate at one point on the track it suggests that there is a fault here and that the derailments were not just unlucky isolated incidents. Similarly, if one engine or wagon collects several markers it would seem that a careful check for the fault is indicated. The necessary repairs or adjustments to the track, locomotives or wagons can then be carried out.

Exhibiting your layout

I am always impressed by the number of model railway exhibitions which are staged, mostly by the many clubs and societies throughout the country, each year. Though some of these shows are disappointing because of poor choice of layouts or bad organisation, most are successful and provide a great deal of pleasure and entertainment, both for model railway enthusiasts and for other members of the general public who visit the shows. It can also be very enjoyable and satisfying for the railway modeller to participate in such exhibitions by showing his or her own layout.

To provide the greatest possible interest the organisers should try to bring together a good variety of different types of layouts, large and small, of differing prototypes, standard and narrow gauge, of different scales, and so on. They should also try to achieve a reasonable balance so that all the visitors will find something of particular interest to them. It is also desirable that the organisers should ensure that all the layouts are of a good standard and that they have not appeared in the same area too often without alterations or additions

having been made. When members of the public are paying for entry I do feel that they have a right to expect that the layouts on display will not be inferior and will not be largely the same ones as at the previous show! It is also important for the club in question in the long term, both for recruitment and for success in staging future shows, that the standards be kept up.

In general the layouts shown fall into two categories, personal and club layouts. The former are usually designed and built purely for the owners' enjoyment and the idea of exhibiting only arises much later. However, some individual modellers have constructed personal layouts with shows in mind. In some cases lack of space at home makes it difficult to operate a model railway and they concentrate more on construction there, taking the opportunity to indulge in some interesting operation while at exhibitions. An example of such a model is Keith Gowen's 'Market Redwing' TT-gauge branch line layout which has been regularly and successfully exhibited in recent years. Keith has little space for a layout

Below *A view of Keith Gowen's TT-gauge branch line layout which was built for exhibition use.* **Right** *A scene on the Bridport branch 00-gauge layout built by the Model Group of the Brooklands Railway Society. Note the effective backscene which not only makes the layout appear larger but also serves to conceal the operators. The road overbridge neatly hides the exit of the track through the backscene to reach the fiddle yard.* **Below right** *A neatly lettered name board completes the exhibition presentation of the Brooklands Railway Society Model Group 00-gauge Bridport branch layout.*

at home so he planned his model railway for exhibition use. The layout was designed so that the four sections which make it up are easy to transport and assemble, and so that they can be conveniently stored in a large cupboard at his home when not in use.

Club layouts are often built specifically for exhibition use by the members. Whether or not the layout was designed for show purposes there are some points to be considered. The layout should be an operating model railway and it should work well. There is a place for static models at exhibitions but layouts should be seen in action. It is preferable that the layout should appear to be complete even if further work is, in fact, still to be carried out later. So, if you have been invited to exhibit your layout this is a good reason for completing any areas of scenery that are as yet unfinished, for building any missing structures, and for adding figures and other details to bring your layout to completion. A possible exception is if you have a particular construction method, for example for scenery, and you wish to show

how this is carried out, perhaps as a series of step by step stages. However, this would probably be best shown as a separate static display in conjunction with your layout, rather than leaving parts of the layout unfinished.

When a layout is on show the presentation is important. Though the surface of the layout may have been properly coloured, detailed and finished, the edges, the framing of the baseboard, may have been left as bare wood. If so a better appearance will result if these edges, after any necessary filling and sanding, are painted with matt black paint. This gives a neat but unobtrusive finish. If your layout lacks a scenic background consider installing one. It will give an impression of greater depth and realism to your scenery and, if you will be operating from behind the layout, the backscene will partly conceal you from the viewers. A backdrop can also be useful for hiding a fiddle yard from view.

Also part of the presentation is a neat name board for your railway. You may also like to provide some explanatory information about

the layout and perhaps a track plan. If your model is based on a particular prototype line, for example a branch line, you might like to feature a display of photographs of the real thing to show visitors what you have modelled. If you are running the layout to a timetable or are following a sequence of operation during the exhibition you may wish to have a copy of the timetable mounted beside the layout so that members of the public can follow the movements that are taking place at any particular time. Prior to the show you will probably be asked to provide some details of your layout and perhaps a track plan for inclusion in the official printed exhibition guide or handbook. Try to cover the things which you would like to know about the layout if it belonged to someone else when you write these brief notes about the model.

If you are invited to show your layout at an exhibition, check on its transportability well before the date of the show. Can it be carried in sections in a car or estate car or will it be necessary to borrow or hire a small van? If you own a car and are planning to build a layout it may be worth while designing it in sections

The Mid Hants Model Railway Group model of the Watlington branch in EM gauge is a portable layout and many of the small details, such as the human figures and the telegraph pole in this view of the station approach, together with the structures, are detachable for storage and transport.

which will fit into your car. If you do not take your layout down very often, try a few practice runs of taking the sections apart and reassembling them so that the process will be quick and easy when you come to set it up at the show. Constructing the layout so that fragile items such as structures and details can be removed for transportation or storage will help to avoid damage. If you do this keep the removable items in boxes or cartons so that they do not get mislaid when not on the layout. The Mid Hants Model Railway Group's exhibition model of the Watlington Branch in EM gauge is a portable layout on which almost all the structures and details, such as telegraph poles, lamps, figures, road vehicles, and so on, can be removed for moving or storing the layout. Each human figure has a wire fitted beneath one foot which fits into a suitably placed hole in the platform or other surface. It is also important to have some means of carrying your locomotives and rolling stock safely to and from the exhibition. This may simply be a cardboard box within which the individual models are placed after wrapping in tissue paper or after putting into their original boxes. If you anticipate attending a number of shows it is worth taking the time to make a wooden carrying case fitted with partitions in appropriate positions and lined with foam rubber to protect the models.

It is a good idea to keep the electrical arrangements for your layout as neat and tidy as possible. This will make it easier to set up and there will be less risk of people getting snagged by the wiring with the danger of disconnecting or damaging it. As you may need assistance from club members in running your layout, particularly when you want to have a break so that you can have a meal or visit the rest of the show, it is helpful if your control arrangements are straightforward and clearly labelled. Thus another operator taking over will be able to run the layout without too much difficulty and without the need for elaborate instructions.

At some exhibitions the lighting is poor. Often the hall is a hired one, not equipped with suitable lighting and there may be little the club can do to provide better illumination. Poor lighting may make it difficult for the visitors to see the detail work on your layout properly and can also give the impression that it is dull and lifeless instead of doing justice to your realistic colouring. It is well worth while fitting effective lights to your layout if you plan to attend a few exhibitions; the lights may also be useful when running the model railway at home. Effective lighting can do a great deal to enhance a model railway but it is an aspect of presentation that

Above *Dick Wyatt has several bright lights which he fixes above the corners of his narrow-gauge layout at shows. These enable the beautifully detailed and coloured scenery and structures to be seen to full advantage. These two pictures were taken at an exhibition and the excellent even illumination is evident.* Below *The control panel of the Mid Hants Model Railway Group EM-gauge model of Watlington station is neatly laid out and fully labelled, making it easy for operators, even those who do not regularly run the layout.*

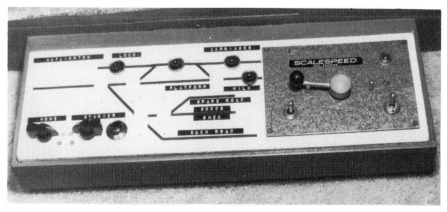

Plate glass or perspex panels provide effective protection for a layout at shows without interfering with viewing, as on this exhibition layout owned by Hestair Models. The top edge of the screen is just visible in this picture as a white line across the lower part.

is often rather neglected. As a temporary exhibition measure even a couple of adjustable reading lamps can be of use on a small layout if positioned to illuminate important parts of the model. An ideal arrangement is to fit fluorescent strip lighting over your layout as this gives even illumination, but this is more suitable for home use than at exhibitions.

At shows there are inevitably visitors usually, though not always, children, who seemingly must touch everything, including your layout, with the risk of damage to small details. Efforts are made at exhibitions to keep the public from getting too close to the layouts, often by putting a row of chairs in front of each layout. This can be reasonably effective but it is difficult to stop children from moving or climbing onto the chairs. If you are planning to attend several shows as an exhibitor you may feel it is worth the effort and cost of fitting perspex panels along the front edge of the layout. These panels of perspex, thick enough to be rigid, should be about 10 or 12 inches high and are very effective in preventing handling of the layout by the public but do not interfere with viewing. They are best fixed in place with screws along the lower edges so that they can be fitted for shows but easily removed when the layout is again set up at home.

Operating models such as cranes, windmills, watermills, and so on seem popular with visitors to model railway shows and you might consider installing one or more on your layout.

Some modellers feel that models of this type are inappropriate on a scale model railway layout, regarding them as gimmicky and toy-like. However the kits available are generally well detailed and realistic models and the extra movement and interest which these working models can add to the scene are of benefit, particularly on a small layout where the train operating potential may be rather limited.

I have already mentioned that it is important to check and prepare the locomotives, rolling stock and track on your layout beforehand so that operation will be as smooth and reliable as possible during the exhibition. Conditions at shows are often unfavourable because of dust and dirt, humidity, and so on. If the show lasts more than one day it is a good idea to clean the track before starting operation each day.

Rather than run the trains at random it is much better to have some system of operation for exhibitions. Haphazard running of the trains may give a toy-like impression to the visitors whereas systematic operation will create a much more realistic effect. Rather than have to decide what you are going to do on the spur of the moment, have a simple sequence arranged and practised beforehand. Try to make this series of train movements interesting and authentic so that visitors will find them realistic and will want to see what happens next. Keep the sequence fairly simple and make sure that you are really familiar with it so that with the distractions of the exhibition you can still remember what you are doing and what you

Above *Operating models add interest and are particularly beneficial on a small layout. This interesting working lift bridge was built from a Pola/Hornby kit. The bridge spans the entrance to a small harbour on an 00-gauge layout.* **Below** *A scene on the Bridport branch 00-gauge layout built by the Model Group of the Brooklands Railway Society. The attractive scenery has been realistically blended with the back scene giving a very spacious effect. Note the card system indicating to viewers the train movements which are taking place. As each is completed the card is flipped over to reveal the next.*

should do next! It is helpful to have a card or a series of cards on which the moves are clearly printed to use as an aid to memory and for the benefit of any assistants or relief operators who are not familiar with operating the layout. The interest of your model railway for the viewers will be enhanced if it is made clear to those watching what train movements are taking place. A convenient method is to have a series of cards with the moves on them. These cards are mounted in a suitable place arranged so that, as each move is completed, the card concerned can be flipped up to reveal the next. Keith Gowen uses this scheme with a convenient variation. In addition to the information on the front of each card intended for the viewer, there are details on the rear for the operator. Any sequence should not be too long so that it can be completed reasonably quickly. There can then be a pause before it is repeated. During this natural break spectators will move away making room for others to take their places to see the layout in action. Equally important, it gives an opportunity for visitors to ask questions and to talk to the operators.

Exhibitions have an important role to play in public relations for railway modelling in encouraging people to take up the hobby and